cycling traffic-free
Midlands and
Peak District

Ian Allan
PUBLISHING

Cycling Traffic Free; Midlands and Peak District
Nick Cotton

First published 2010

ISBN 978 0 7110 3469 3

Published by Ian Allan Publishing

An imprint of Ian Allan Publishing Ltd, Hersham, Surrey KT12 4RG.
Printed in England by Ian Allan Printing Ltd, Hersham, Surrey KT12 4RG.

Visit the Ian Allan Publishing website at www.ianallanpublishing.com

Distributed in the United States of America and Canada by BookMasters Distribution
Services.

Code 1007/D3

CONTENTS

THE MAIN ROUTES

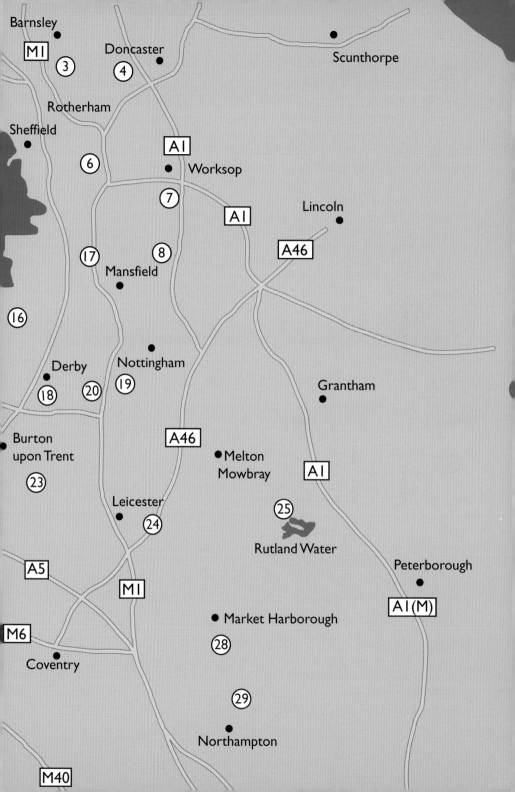

INTRODUCTION

More and more people are realising that cycling is good for their health and well-being. The government has started showing a real interest in promoting cycling as a way of solving transport problems, and the National Cycle Network is having a major effect on helping to change lifestyles and people's mode of transport. However, vehicle numbers are still increasing which means that even minor lanes can become busy with traffic – you can rarely be guaranteed to find the safety, peace and quiet that are the essential ingredients of a family bike ride on the road network.

This book describes 30 routes, many of them easy and waymarked, where you can cycle free from traffic, and gives further information about where else to find enjoyable rides and how to obtain information produced by local authorities and other organisations.

OTHER ROUTES IN BRIEF

In addition to the 30 main rides featured in the book, there are many other routes in the area which are worth a brief mention:

BARNSLEY, ROTHERHAM, SHEFFIELD AND SURROUNDS

Barnsley Canal

The Trans Pennine Trail uses a 4½-mile section of the disused Barnsley Canal, passing some atmospheric rock cuttings between Walton and Royston (due north of Barnsley). www.penninewaterways.co.uk/barnsley
www.transpenninetrail.org.uk

Barnsley link to Trans Pennine Trail

Starting from the A628 Cudworth road, about ½ mile southeast of Barnsley railway station, a 2-mile traffic-free spur links via Stairfoot to the Dove Trail at its eastern end (Wombwell). www.transpenninetrail.org.uk

Rotherham to Sheffield

An 8-mile trail runs south from Rotherham railway station alongside the River Don then the Sheffield & Keadby Canal to join the Five Weirs Walk near Meadowhall and continue into central Sheffield.
www.sheffield.gov.uk/roads-and-transport and follow links to 'Cycling' and 'Cycle maps'.

Wharncliffe Woods

A spur from the Trans Pennine Trail climbs the steep slopes of Wharncliffe Woods before dropping down to Sheffield. There are also waymarked routes in the woods.
www.wharncliffe.info
www.mtbbritain.co.uk/wharncliffe_woods.html

BIRMINGHAM AND SURROUNDS
Birmingham Canals
As well as the Birmingham Main Line and the Worcester & Birmingham Canal (described in Ride 27) the Birmingham & Fazeley Canal can be followed east from Gas Street Basin under Spaghetti Junction (a bizarre but well-recommended experience) as far as Minworth.
www.waterscape.com/canals-and-rivers/birmingham-and-fazeley-canal

Rea Valley Route
A 5-mile traffic-free trail runs southwest from Cannon Hill Park (near Edgbaston) to Northfield railway station. www.birmingham.gov.uk and follow links through 'Transport and Streets' to 'Cycle Routes'.

Sutton Park
Several routes are possible in this large park located 5 five miles north of Birmingham city centre. www.birmingham.gov.uk/suttonpark.bcc

CAMBRIDGESHIRE
Grafham Water, west of Cambridge
A 7-mile circuit of the reservoir, although little time is actually spent by the water's edge. www.anglianwater.co.uk/leisure/what-to-see/water-parks/grafham

Peterborough
There is a good 7-mile route through Peterborough from Ferry Meadows in the west to Flag Fen and Shanks Millennium Bridge in the east.
www.peterborough.gov.uk and follow links through 'traffic, travel and parking' then 'Travel Choice' to 'Cycling'. www.pect.org.uk/green-wheel

CHESHIRE
Middlewood Way
A 10-mile railway path from Marple, on the southeast edge of Manchester, south to Macclesfield. Long sections are very muddy after rain and throughout the winter.
www.macclesfield-outdoors.co.uk/places/middlewoodway.html
www.cheshireeast.gov.uk/leisure_and_culture and search 'Middlewood Way'.

Salt Line, east of Crewe
A short railway path route from Hassall Green to Alsager, northwest of Stoke, easily linked to the Trent & Mersey Canal.
www.cheshire.gov.uk/countryside/OutandAbout/linear_trails/salt_line.htm

Tatton Park, north of Knutsford
Plenty of options to explore the estate roads and offroad tracks in this beautifully landscaped property southwest of Manchester.
www.tattonpark.org.uk

Whitegate Way, west of Northwich
A 7-mile railway path running between Winsford and Cuddington.
www.cheshire.gov.uk/countryside/OutandAbout/linear_trails/whitegate_way.htm

DERBYSHIRE
Elvaston Country Park, east of Derby
A route follows the River Derwent from the centre of Derby to Elvaston Country Park where several circuits are possible.
www.cyclederby.co.uk/routes/leisure-routes

Etwall to Mickleover, west of Derby
A section of National Cycle Network Route 54 to the west of Derby, linking Etwall to Mickleover along the course of an old railway.
www.cyclederby.co.uk/routes/leisure-routes

Monsal Trail, Bakewell
A short railway path in the heart of the Peak District, starting near Bakewell.
www.visitderbyshire.co.uk/Activities. Scroll down to 'Cycling in and around Derbyshire'

Sett Valley Trail, east of Stockport
A short railway path from Hayfield, on the edge of the Peak District, southeast of Manchester. www.visitderbyshire.co.uk/Activities. Scroll down to 'Cycling in and around Derbyshire'

LEICESTERSHIRE
Market Harborough Arm of the Grand Union Canal
A 6-mile length of canal towpath meanders northwest from Market Harborough to Foxton Locks.
www.waterscape.com/canals-and-rivers/grand-union-canal-leicester-line

LINCOLNSHIRE
Lincoln
A 25-mile railway path route from Harby and Skellingthorpe in the west, through the centre of Lincoln to Bardney and Woodhall Spa in the east.
www.woodhallspa.org/leisure_waterrailway.html
www.lincolnshire.gov.uk and search 'Cycling routes'.

MANCHESTER AND SURROUNDS
Sale Water Park, south Manchester
Part of the Trans Pennine Trail through Manchester, there are plenty of circuits possible in this expanse of lakes and parkland. www.merseyvalley.org.uk and click on 'Sites'.

NOTTINGHAMSHIRE
Clumber Park to Blidworth, east of Mansfield
A section of National Cycle Network Route 6, using a mix of forest trails and bridleways. www.nottinghamshire.gov.uk/manashcycle.pdf

Newark railway path
A 5-mile railway path leading directly south from Newark railway station to Cotham. www.nottinghamshire.gov.uk/newarkcycleguide.pdf

Southwell Trail, east of Mansfield
An 8-mile railway path leading northwest from Southwell, with its fine minster, to Bilsthorpe. www.nottinghamshire.gov.uk/manashcycle.pdf

Shipley Country Park, west of Nottingham
A country park west of Nottingham with many possible circuits. The Nutbrook Trail (Ride 20) links Long Eaton to Shipley Country Park. www.derbyshire-peakdistrict.co.uk/shipleypark.htm

SHROPSHIRE
Shropshire woodlands
There are several small woodlands in Shropshire with waymarked routes. www.forestry.gov.uk/marches

STAFFORDSHIRE
Churnet Valley Trail, east of Stoke
A 4-mile railway path between Denstone and Oakamoor, right next to Alton Towers. www.staffordshire.gov.uk/transport/walkingandcycling/maps You will need the map covering Staffordshire Moorlands.

Rudyard Lake
A waymarked route on cyclepaths and quiet streets from the centre of Leek to Rudyard Lake, running alongside a miniature railway. www.rudyardlake.com

Stafford to Newport Greenway
A railway path running west from Stafford to Haughton.
There are plans for it to be extended further west to Newport.
www.staffordshire.gov.uk/transport/walkingandcycling/maps
You will need the map covering Stafford.

Stoke
Two rides from Stoke are described in the main section (Rides 11 and & 14).
Another option is National Cycle Network Route 5 which uses sections of the
Trent & Mersey Canal, a railway path and parkland on a route between the centre
of Stoke and Alsager, to the northwest of the city.
www.stoke.gov.uk/cycling
www.stoke.gov.uk/ccm/navigation/leisure/cycle-routes

WIRRAL
North Wirral Coastal Path
A ride along the promenade from New Brighton to Hoylake.
www.wirral.gov.uk and search 'Wirral Cycle Map'.

The Wirral Way
A 12-mile railway path northwest from Hooton parallel with the Dee estuary to
West Kirby. www.discovercheshire.co.uk/files/PDF/routepacks/wirral_way.pdf

WORCESTERSHIRE
Stourport Canal
Good quality canal towpath from Stourport north to Kidderminster.
www.waterscape.com/in-your-area/worcestershire/stourport
www.canaljunction.com/canal/staffs_worcs.htm

Worcester
There are several routes radiating out from the centre of Worcester: a circuit around
the perimeter of the race course; a linear ride along the west side of the River Severn;
and a 6-mile section of the Worcester & Birmingham Canal northeast to Tibberton.
www.worcestershire.gov.uk/home/wcc-transport-cycleleisureguides

Wyre Forest
There is a waymarked forestry route starting from the attractive visitor centre in
Wyre Forest, to the northwest of Bewdley.
www.worcestershire.whub.org.uk and search 'Cycling'

TOURIST INFORMATION CENTRES

Tourist Information Centres often stock a good range of cycling information in the form of leaflets, maps and guidebooks. If you need a leaflet they will often be able to send it to you more quickly than the council which has produced and published it.

Cheshire

Chester	01244 402111
Congleton	01260 271095
Ellesmere Port	0151 356 7879
Knutsford	01565 632611
Macclesfield	01625 504114
Nantwich	01270 610983
Northwich	01606 353534
Runcorn	0151 907 8303
Warrington	01925 428585
Wilmslow	01625 522275

Derbyshire

Ashbourne	01335 343666
Bakewell	01629 816558
Buxton	01298 25106
Chesterfield	01246 345777
Derby	01332 255802
Glossop	01457 855920
Matlock	01629 583388
Matlock Bath	01629 550082
Ripley	01773 841488
Swadlincote	01283 222848

Leicestershire

Ashby de la Zouch	01530 411767
Hinckley	01455 635106
Leicester	0844 888 5181
Loughborough	01509 218113
Market Harborough	01858 828282
Rutland Water	01572 653026

Northamptonshire

Brackley	01280 700111
Corby	01536 407507
Kettering	01536 410266
Northampton	01604 838800
Oundle	01832 274333
Rushden	01832 742189

Nottinghamshire

Newark	01636 655765
Nottingham	0844 477 5678
Ollerton	01623 824545
Retford	01777 860780
Worksop	01909 501148

Shropshire

Bridgnorth	01746 763257
Church Stretton	01694 723133
Ellesmere	01691 622981
Ironbridge	01952 884391
Ludlow	01584 875053
Market Drayton	01630 653114
Much Wenlock	01952 727679
Oswestry	01691 662753
Shrewsbury	01743 281200
Telford	01952 238008
Whitchurch	01948 664577

Staffordshire

Burton upon Trent	01283 508111
Cannock	01543 877666
Leek	01538 483741
Lichfield	01543 412121
Newcastle-under-Lyme	01782 297313
Stafford	01785 619619
Stoke-on-Trent	01782 236000
Tamworth	01827 709581

Warwickshire

Kenilworth	01926 748900
Leamington Spa	0870 160 7930
Nuneaton	02476 347006
Rugby	01788 533217
Stratford-upon-Avon	0870 160 7930
Warwick	01926 492212

West Midlands

Birmingham	0844 888 3883
Birmingham	0870 225 0127
Coventry	024 7622 5616
Merry Hill	01384 487900
Solihull	0121 704 6130
Walsall	01922 653110
Wolverhampton	01902 556110

Worcestershire

Bewdley	01299 404740
Broadway	01386 852937
Bromsgrove	01527 831809
Droitwich Spa	01905 774312
Evesham	01386 446944
Malvern	01684 892289
Pershore	01386 556591
Redditch	01527 60806
Tenbury Wells	01584 810136
Upton upon Severn	01684 594200
Worcester	01905 726311

Yorkshire

Barnsley	01226 206757
Doncaster	01302 734309
Huddersfield	01484 223200
Rotherham	01709 835904
Sheffield	0114 221 1900

USEFUL WEBSITES

More and more cycling information is being made available on the internet and the better websites are constantly being upgraded. If you are prepared to search for 'Cycling', 'Cycle routes' or 'Cycle maps' on local authority websites you will normally find details of routes, leaflets and maps, some of which you will be able to download and print off at home.

Cheshire
www.cheshire.gov.uk/cycling/
www.visitcheshire.com/site/things-to-do/outdoor-pursuits/cycling
www.discovercheshire.co.uk and follow 'Cycling' links.

Derbyshire
www.visitderbyshire.co.uk/fa_cycling.ihtml
www.derbyshire.gov.uk/transport_roads/road_safety/bicycles/cycling_routes/default.asp
www.derbyshire-peakdistrict.co.uk/cycling.htm

Leicestershire
www.leics.gov.uk/index/environment/countryside/cycle_trails.htm
www.leicester.gov.uk and follow 'Transport & Streets' to 'Cycling'.

Northamptonshire
www.northamptonshire.gov.uk and follow links through 'Transport & Streets' to 'Walking & Cycling'.

Nottinghamshire
www.nottinghamshire.gov.uk/home/leisure/l-cycling.htm
www.visitnottingham.com and follow links through 'Things to do' to 'Activities' and 'Cycling'.

Shropshire
www.shropshirecycling.co.uk
www.shropshire.gov.uk/cycling.nsf
www.cycleshropshire.org.uk
www.shropshiretourism.co.uk/cycling

Staffordshire
www.staffordshire.gov.uk/transport/walkingandcycling/maps
www.cyclestaffordshire.co.uk

Warwickshire
www.warwickshire.gov.uk and search 'Cycling' or go via 'Roads & Travel' to 'Cycling'.

Worcestershire
www.visitworcestershire.org and search for 'Cycling'.

Yorkshire
www.transpenninetrail.org.uk

WHERE TO CYCLE TRAFFIC-FREE IN THE MIDLANDS AND PEAK DISTRICT

In general, traffic-free cycling routes can be divided into six categories:
*   dismantled railways
*   Forestry Commission routes
*   waterside routes: canal towpaths, riverside routes, and reservoirs
*   country parks and National Trust properties
*   routes created by local authorities, often as part of the National Cycle Network
*   the Rights of Way network

DISMANTLED RAILWAYS

The vast majority of Britain's railway system was built in the 50 years from 1830 to 1880. After the invention of the car and the development of the road network from the turn of the 20th century onwards, the railways went into decline and in the 1960s many of the lines were closed and the tracks lifted. This was the famous 'Beeching Axe'. It is a great tragedy that Dr Beeching was not a keen leisure cyclist! Had he set in motion the development of leisure trails along the course of the railways he was so busy closing, we could boast one of the finest recreational cycling networks in the world.

As it is, many of the railways were sold off in small sections to adjacent landowners and the continuity of long sections of dismantled track was lost. Almost 50 years on, some local authorities have risen to the challenge and created some fine trails along the course of the dismantled railways. Within this book more than half of the routes use old railways.

Dismantled railways make good cycle trails for two reasons: first, the gradients tend to be very gentle and, second, the broad stone base is ideal for creating a smooth firm surface for bicycles.

FORESTRY COMMISSION ROUTES

There are three Forestry Commission holdings with waymarked routes described as main rides in this book:

1. Sherwood Pines Forest Park (Ride 8)
2. Delamere Forest, near Chester (Ride 10)
3. Cannock Chase, near Stafford (Ride 22)

There are also many smaller woodlands in Shropshire where it is easy to devise your own routes. The Forestry Commission website www.forestry.gov.uk is an excellent source of information about cycling and mountain biking.

WATERSIDE ROUTES: CANAL TOWPATHS, RIVERSIDE ROUTES AND RESERVOIRS

The British Waterways Board undertook a national survey of its 2,000 miles of towpath to see what percentage was suitable for cycling. Unfortunately the results were not very encouraging – less than a fifth meet the specified requirements. The rest are too narrow, rutted, overgrown or pass under many low bridges. In certain cases regional water companies have co-ordinated with local authorities to improve the towpaths for all users. It is to be hoped that this collaboration continues and extends throughout the country.

Cycling along canal towpaths can provide plenty of interest – wildlife, barges and locks – and the gradient tends to be flat. However, even the best quality towpaths are not places to cycle fast as they are often busy with anglers and walkers and it is rare that cycling two abreast is feasible. For more information go to the British Waterways website www.waterscape.com. As for other rides beside water, the most important reservoirs for cycling in the area covered by the book are:

1. Upper Derwent Reservoirs (Ride 5)
2. Carsington Water (Ride 16)
3. Rutland Water (Ride 25)
4. Pitsford Water (Ride 29)

COUNTRY PARKS AND NATIONAL TRUST PROPERTIES

There are many country parks and National Trust properties where cycle routes have been waymarked. To find country parks it is best to go via the local authority website and put 'country parks' into the search box. For National Trust properties go to www.nationaltrust.org.uk

ROUTES CREATED BY LOCAL AUTHORITIES

By using a mixture of quiet lanes and improved footpaths and bridleways local authorities can signpost and promote a route to make the most of existing networks. These include much of the Trans Pennine Trail and large sections of the National Cycle Network – see www.sustrans.org.uk

THE RIGHTS OF WAY NETWORK

If you wish to venture beyond the relatively protected world of cycle trails you can devise your own route. Study the relevant Ordnance Survey Landranger map: the yellow roads criss-crossing the countryside represent the smaller quieter lanes. When cycling offroad you must stay on legal rights of way: it is illegal to cycle on footpaths, but you are allowed to use bridleways, byways open to all traffic (BOATs) and roads used as public paths (RUPPs). These are all marked on Ordnance Survey maps. Devising routes 'blind' can sometimes be a bit of a hit-or-miss affair, however. Some tracks may turn out to be muddy or overgrown. It often takes several outings to devise the best possible offroad route that starts right from your front door. Expect the riding conditions to change radically from the height of summer to the depths of winter.

SUSTRANS AND THE NATIONAL CYCLE NETWORK

The National Cycle Network is a linked series of traffic-free paths and traffic-calmed roads being developed right across the United Kingdom, linking town centres and the countryside. Visit Sustrans' website www.sustrans.org.uk for more details of the five main National Cycle Network long distance routes in the region covered by this book:

1. South Midlands Cycle Route
2. West Midlands Cycle Route
3. Derby to York
4. Pennine Cycleway
5. The Trans Pennine Trail

THE COUNTRY CODE

- Enjoy the countryside and respect its life and work
- Guard against all risk of fire
- Fasten all gates
- Keep your dogs under close control
- Keep to rights of way across farmland
- Use gates and stiles to cross fences, hedges and walls
- Leave livestock, crops and machinery alone
- Take your litter home
- Help to keep all water clean
- Protect wildlife, plants and trees
- Take special care on country roads
- Make no unnecessary noise

Cycling Traffic-Free:
Midlands and the Peak District
The Main Routes

ROUTE 1
Longdendale Trail, northeast of Glossop

Distance: 6½ miles one way, 13 miles return.
Map/leaflet: Ordnance Survey Landranger map 110. *Trans Pennine Trail Map 1 – Irish Sea to Yorkshire* shows this and several other routes in the area. Go to www.transpenninetrail.org.uk
Websites: www.derbyshireuk.net/longdendale_trail.html and www.transpenninetrail.org.uk
Hills: Steady climb (330ft/100m) from Hadfield to the Woodhead Tunnel.
Surface: Good stone-based track.
Roads and road crossings: The B6105 is crossed about halfway along the trail. If you choose to continue eastwards on the tough link to Dunford Bridge you will also need to cross the busy A628.
Refreshments: None on the route itself; the nearest are in Padfield or Hadfield.

Starting from Hadfield (the location for the TV series *The League of Gentlemen*) the Longdendale Trail climbs gently from predominantly wooded cuttings and embankments to open moorland with fine views ahead of the Pennines and down to the left of the string of reservoirs in the valley below. The surface is a mixture of fine gravel with the occasional rougher stony section. The trail is part of the much longer Trans Pennine Trail which crosses the country from the west coast at Southport to the North Sea at Hornsea, northeast of Hull. It is possible to continue east to the highest point of the Trans Pennine Trail then descend towards Penistone, but this involves a much steeper climb on rougher tracks.

BACKGROUND AND PLACES OF INTEREST
The old Railway
The railway through Longdendale provided the first rail link between Manchester and Sheffield. A passenger service started in 1845 and ran for 136 years until 1981. The Woodhead Tunnel was one of the great achievements of the early years of the railway age. North West Water purchased the railway line in 1989 and used the ballast in a major engineering project to raise the Woodhead Dam as a flood safety measure. Once the dam works were complete, clearance work began on the track, followed by major landscaping and drainage works.

The reservoirs
The five reservoirs of Bottoms, Valehouse, Rhodeswood, Torside and Woodhead were completed in 1877 and formed the largest artificial expanse of water in the world at the time.

Starting Points & Parking:
1. **Hadfield** and **Padfield** are well signposted off the A57 Manchester to Glossop road. Climb through the centre of Hadfield following 'Longdendale Trail' signs, then just before the railway bridge over the road there is a car park to the left at the start of the trail (Grid reference SK 025962).

2. **Woodhead Tunnel/Woodhead Reservoir:** there is a car park at the eastern end of the trail off the A628 about 1 mile east of its junction with the A6024 Holmfirth road (Grid reference SK 112999). This can be accessed only from the east and is not well signposted.

3. **Along the B6105:** there are several small car parking areas close to the trail just off this road along the south side of the reservoirs.

ROUTE INSTRUCTIONS

1. From the Hadfield car park follow the access ramp up to the trail and through a wooded section.
2. After 2½ miles you will need to cross the B6105 – follow signs for 'Trans Pennine Trail – East' to cross the road at the safest point.
3. After a further 2 miles there is a short steep climb to pass beneath power lines and arrive at the start of the final reservoir (Woodhead).
4. The trail ends 6½ miles from Hadfield at the gated entrance to the Woodhead Tunnels.

The Trans Pennine Trail can be followed eastwards but the going becomes steep and rough, involving two crossings of the busy A628 then a long descent on road. The next traffic-free section to the east runs from Dunford Bridge to Penistone (see Ride 2)

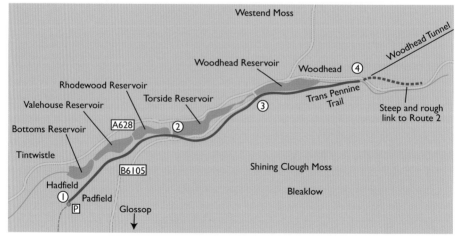

Distance: (a) Penistone to Dunford Bridge – 6 miles one way, 12 miles return; (b) Penistone to the A616 – 4½ miles one way, 9 miles return.

Map/leaflet: Ordnance Survey Landranger map 110. *Trans Pennine Trail Map 2 – Derbyshire & Yorkshire* shows this and several other routes in the area. See website below.

Website: www.transpenninetrail.org.uk

Hills: There is a steady climb northwest from the A616 near Wortley through Penistone to Dunford Bridge and a steady descent in the other direction, i.e. it will be easier cycling east than cycling west!

Surface: A variety – from tarmac (through Penistone) to stone and gravel with some puddles and surface mud after rain and through the winter.

Roads and road crossings: No dangerous crossings.

Refreshments: Lots of choice in Penistone; pub just off the route in Oxspring.

The route – part of the Trans Pennine Trail – crosses the Pennines between Longdendale and Dunford Bridge, passing above the Woodhead Tunnels which used to carry the railway line. So from Dunford Bridge (at 985ft/300m) down to the end of the ride at the River Don south of Thurgoland (at 490ft/150m) there is a drop of 500 ft over almost 11 miles. Take into account the likelihood of the wind blowing from the west and you soon see that it is normally a lot quicker heading east downhill with the wind behind you than heading west uphill into the wind! Penistone is an attractive stone-built town with plenty of choices of refreshment. Heading west from here the views are of drystone walls and sheep-grazed moorland in the Upper Don Valley. Dunford Bridge is the turnaround point. To the east of Penistone the trail is increasingly wooded as it loses height. The ride could easily be linked either to Ride 3, the Dove Valley Trail, by following the Trans Pennine Trail signs from Oxspring to Silkstone Common, or alternatively continuing south on the track that climbs up into Wharncliffe Woods, taking you to Grenoside, perched high above Sheffield.

BACKGROUND AND PLACES OF INTEREST

Penistone
A busy market town with a 13th-century church. The Cloth Hall and Shambles date from the late 18th century.

Starting Points & Parking:
1. **Dunford Bridge:** on a minor road off the B6106 about 6 miles west of Penistone (Grid reference SE 159024).
2. **Penistone:** about 7 miles west of Barnsley on the A628 (west of M1 Jct 37). Follow signs for the free car park in Penistone, just west of the main part of the village, near to the market (Grid reference SE 245034).
3. **West of Wortley:** the Equine Centre (Grid reference SK 299994).
4. **Wharncliffe Woods:** north of Grenoside (Grid reference SK 326950).

ROUTE INSTRUCTIONS:

The route is well signposted as the Trans Pennine Trail or the Upper Don Trail. From the free car park in Penistone, join the railway path and either:

1. Turn left (west) for Dunford Bridge (6 miles, gentle 300ft/90m climb)
2. Turn right (east) towards Wharncliffe and Sheffield as far as the A616 (4½ miles, gentle 200ft/60m descent). After 3 miles you will pass through the long, lit tunnel at Thurgoland which has the most amazing echo!

Trans Pennine Trail south to Grenoside via Wharncliffe Woods

A wide stone-based forestry track continues south from the A616 through Wharncliffe Woods for a further 5½ miles. This is a tough rollercoaster route with several short, steep climbs and one long final climb (450ft/140m) up to the car park in Grenoside. There are also mountain bike trails in the woods.

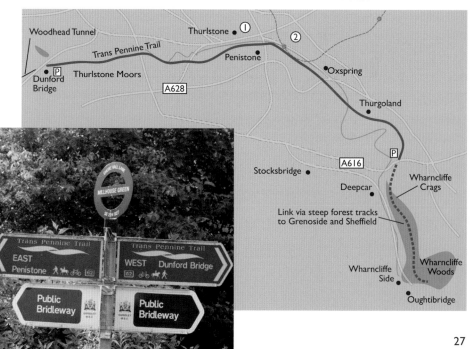

27

ROUTE 3
Dove Valley Trail, south of Barnsley

Distance: (a) Silkstone Common to Worsbrough Country Park – 4½ miles; (b) Worsbrough Country Park to Old Moor Wetland Centre – 6 miles.

Map/leaflet: Ordnance Survey Landranger maps 110 & 111. *Trans Pennine Trail Map 2 – Derbyshire & Yorkshire* shows this and several other routes in the area. See website below.

Website: www.transpenninetrail.org.uk

Hills: The trail descends 525ft/160m east from Silkstone Common down to the Old Moor Wetland Centre.

Surface: Mix of good quality gravel tracks, short stretches of tarmac and the odd short rougher section which may have puddles and mud after rain or in winter.

Roads and road crossings: Where the trail is at road level the busy roads are crossed via toucan crossings; care should be taken at the minor road crossings.

Refreshments: Pub at Silkstone Common (just off the route); Boatman's Rest pub on the southeast side of Worsbrough (just off the route); café at the Old Moor Wetland Visitor Centre.

Passing through the rolling countryside to the south of Barnsley, it is gratifying to see the enormous efforts that have been made to transform the ugly spoil heaps and wastelands of the coal mining industry into green and wooded areas and a wetland nature reserve (the Old Moor Wetland Centre) with man-made lakes attracting a wide variety of wildfowl. Here is a real case of nature being actively encouraged to heal over scars and one wonders whether any present inhabitant would recognise the place in 50 years' time when the trees have had a chance to mature and the hard edges of the massive earth-moving operations have been softened by the growth of grass and wildflowers. Barnsley is the headquarters of the Trans Pennine Trail and there is a link from here to the Dove Valley Trail at Wombwell. It is also possible to continue further east on the Trans Pennine Trail linking to Ride 4.

BACKGROUND AND PLACES OF INTEREST
History of the railway
The Worsbrough Bank Railway was opened in 1880 to allow large amounts of Lancashire-bound coal traffic to bypass the serious bottleneck of Barnsley. The Bank included 2½ miles of 1 in 40 gradient, one of the steepest gradients in the country and a severe obstacle to heavily laden westbound coal trains. In 1952, the line was electrified, one of the first such schemes in Britain. The 142-minute journey from Wath to Dunford Bridge was whittled down to 66 minutes! The track was closed in 1981.

Starting Points & Parking:
1. **Worsbrough Mill Country Park:** 3 miles north of Jct 36 of the M1, along the A61 towards Barnsley. The Trans Pennine Trail crosses the A61 about 200 yards north of the exit to the car park (Grid reference SE 353034). There is also a car park right on the trail itself on the minor road west of Worsbrough towards the M1 and Hood Green (Grid reference SE 344037).
2. **Old Moor Wetland Centre:** near the junction of the A6195 and A633 to the southeast of Barnsley (Grid reference SE 423022).

ROUTE INSTRUCTIONS

The route is well signposted as the Trans Pennine Trail (or the Dove Valley Trail west of Wombwell) and is easily accessed from either of the starting points mentioned above.

Worsbrough west to Silkstone Common

1. Follow 'Trans Pennine Trail West' signs, climbing gently for 4½ miles, crossing the M1 after 1½ miles. The trail runs along the bed of the old railway as far as Silkstone Common, then on a narrower path on the top of the embankment through woodland.
2. It is suggested you turn around when you come to a T-junction with a wider, rougher stone track by a gate and a wooden seat (Grid reference SE 283036). Following the Trans Pennine Trail west from here involves steep gradients, roads and some rougher tracks to link to the Upper Don Trail in Oxspring (see Ride 2).

Worsbrough east to the Old Moor Wetland Centre

3. Follow 'Trans Pennine Trail East' signs, soon crossing the busy A61 via a toucan crossing. After 1½ miles pass beneath a railway viaduct then keep bearing right to cross two bridges over the A633.
4. A track from Barnsley joins from the left (remember this point for your return).
5. Go past Wombwell Football Club ground. Cross into the Old Moor Wetland Reserve (there is a good café here, just off the route). For a longer ride, link to Ride 4 and continue east to Sprotbrough.

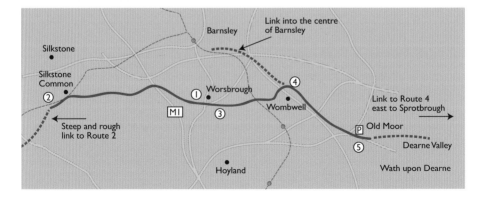

Distance: 10 miles one way, 20 miles return.

Map/leaflet: Ordnance Survey Landranger map 111. *Trans Pennine Trail Map 2 – Derbyshire & Yorkshire* shows this and several other routes in the area. See website below.

Website: www.transpenninetrail.org.uk

Hills: There are several gentle hills and one steeper one to climb from the riverside up onto the massive railway viaduct over the River Don.

Surface: Mix of good quality gravel tracks, short stretches of tarmac and the odd short rougher section which may have puddles and mud after rain or during the winter.

Roads and road crossings: One road to cross (near Dearne Bridge). There is a short section on road through Harlington.

Refreshments: Café at the Old Moor Wetland Visitor Centre; Harlington Inn, Harlington; Boat Inn, Sprotbrough.

Continuing east along the Trans Pennine Trail from the Old Moor Wetland Reserve, this ride is dominated by two rivers: the Dearne and the Don. Year by year the trail is being improved and realigned closer to the two rivers, offering an ever more attractive route through a land reinvented and remodelled after decades of heavy industry. The ruins of Conisbrough Castle, dating back to Norman times, can be seen on the horizon from the trail. The wooded section alongside the Don from Sprotbrough to the enormous viaduct over the river is one of the loveliest on the whole of the coast-to-coast trail. The Boat Inn at Sprotbrough offers a welcome opportunity of refreshment.

NB: There is a short section on road through Harlington where extra care should be taken.

BACKGROUND AND PLACES OF INTEREST
The Don Valley

The River Don was once a major route for transporting goods across the country, and water traffic still uses the river near Sprotbrough. The valley has a richly interwoven industrial and ecological heritage. Sprotbrough Flash, an expanse of open water, was created by subsidence from coal mining at Cadeby and Denaby Main. It sustains over-wintering birds such as little grebes, mute swans and tufted ducks. The great crested grebe returned to the Flash in the 1950s after an absence of almost 100 years. Sir Walter Scott worked on his novel *Ivanhoe* whilst staying at the Boat Inn in Sprotbrough.

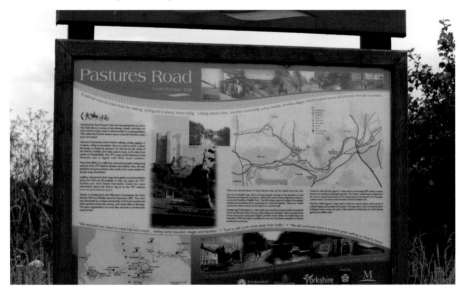

Starting Points & Parking:

1. **Old Moor Wetland Centre:** near the junction of the A6195 and A633 to the southeast of Barnsley (Grid reference SE 423022).
2. **Sprotbrough, west of Doncaster:** small public car park near to the Boat Inn by the River Don on the south side of the village (Grid reference SE 537015).

ROUTE INSTRUCTIONS

The route is well signposted as the Trans Pennine Trail.

Old Moor Wetland Centre east to Sprotbrough

1. Follow 'Trans Pennine Trail East' signs, past the lakes of the wetland centre. After 1½ miles at the road junction go straight ahead onto a continuation of the path.
2. After almost 1 mile, at the next road turn right to pass under the railway bridge then immediately left, signposted 'National Cycle Network Route 62'.
3. Cross a footbridge over the River Dearne, then after ¼ mile – at a crossroads of tracks – turn right. Join the road, bear left then take the first road right, signposted 'Sprotbrough 4'. Go past the Harlington Inn and as the road swings left, turn right onto Mill Lane (no through road) to the river. Turn left along the embankment.
4. Cross a road onto a continuation of the trail, cross a bridge over the River Dearne, climb and go past the old Earth Centre.
5. Drop down to the River Don alongside a huge brick viaduct. Turn left alongside the river for almost 2 miles to the Boat Inn at Sprotbrough.

This traffic-free section of the Trans Pennine Trail can be followed further east then north as far as Bentley where it ends abruptly. There are also signposted links into Doncaster.

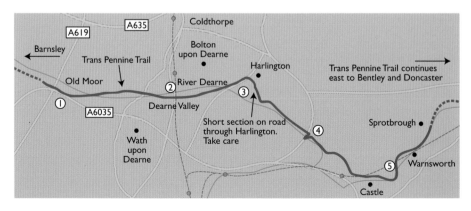

ROUTE 5
Derwent Reservoirs, west of Sheffield

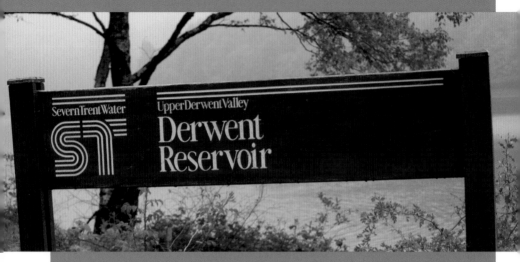

Distance: Two loops, of 11 miles and 5 miles. The upper loop (11 miles) around Derwent and Howden Reservoirs is not only longer but also runs over rougher terrain at the far northeast section of the ride. An easier alternative would be to go out and back along the road that runs along the west side of the reservoirs.

Map/leaflet: Ordnance Survey Landranger map 110.

Website: www.peakdistrict-nationalpark.info

Hills: Several small climbs. The packhorse bridge at Slippery Stones is 270ft (80m) higher than the visitor centre.

Surface: This varies from tarmac to smooth gravel forest track to a rougher track on the east side of Howden Reservoir, where a mountain bikes are recommended.

Roads and road crossings: Vehicles are allowed to use the road on the western side of the reservoirs during the week but not at the weekends. There is traffic on the approach road from the A57 to the visitor centre but there is also a pavement.

Refreshments: At the visitor centre.

Cycle Hire: Available at Fairholmes Visitor Centre (01433 651261).

This wonderful ride is set in the middle of the outstanding natural beauty of woodland, lakes and moorland alongside the series of reservoirs in the Upper Derwent Valley. There are various options of single or double circuits or there-and-back rides. Choosing the right option for you will depend on fitness, weather, the types of bikes you are riding and whether you are prepared to spend any time on roads with traffic. The easiest option would be to follow the road alongside the western edge of Derwent Reservoir, passing the ornate square stone towers at the dams and turning around when you have had enough. The most strenuous would be to do a full circuit of all three reservoirs. Take your pick!

BACKGROUND AND PLACES OF INTEREST
The reservoirs
At the end of the 19th century it was decided that the Upper Derwent Valley would make an ideal location for a reservoir to supply the cities of Sheffield, Nottingham, Derby and Leicester. With its deep narrow valley making dam-building relatively easy, its high annual rainfall, soft water and a moorland catchment area free from the threat of contamination, it was an obvious choice. The dams which created the Howden and Derwent Reservoirs were built between 1901 and 1916 and up to 1,000 people lived in the self-contained workers' village at Birchinlee. The third dam, to create the Ladybower Reservoir, was built between 1935 and 1945.

The Dam Busters Raid
In the weeks leading up to the famous raid on Germany in 1943, the Upper Derwent reservoirs were frequently used for practice by the 617 Squadron, as the topography of the dams was similar to the targets in Germany.

Starting Points & Parking:
Fairholmes Visitor Centre: pay & display car park at the top end of Ladybower Reservoir. Turn off the A57 Sheffield to Glossop road just by the west side of the viaduct over Ladybower Reservoir. Continue for 2½ miles to the car park at the visitor centre (Grid reference SK 173894).

Free car parks: there are free car parks on the approach road to the visitor centre and also one on the east side of Ladybower Reservoir off the A6013 Bamford Road (Grid reference SK 203857).

ROUTE INSTRUCTIONS

Described below is a full clockwise circuit of all three lakes, starting from the visitor centre. The tracks on the east side of the reservoirs are suitable only for mountain bikes. An easier there-and-back ride follows the tarmac road on the west side of Derwent Reservoir to its end alongside the northern arm of the Howden Reservoir.

1. From Fairholmes Visitor Centre, turn right (north) on the tarmac lane alongside Derwent Reservoir, keeping the water to your right. Follow this for 5 miles to the end of the tarmac.
2. At the fork of tracks about ¾ mile beyond the end of the tarmac follow the 'Slippery Stones Cycle Route' sign to cross the River Derwent via the bridge and keep following signs for 'Cycle Trail', soon turning to head south.
3. After a further 4½ miles, at a T-junction shortly after rejoining tarmac at the southern end of Derwent Reservoir, you have the option of turning sharp right

to return to the visitor centre (signposted 'Fairholmes Cycle Hire') or of continuing straight ahead for the full circuit.

4. (Full circuit) The tarmac turns to track after 1 mile and follows the east side of Ladybower Reservoir. At the T-junction with the busy A57 turn right on the shared-use pavement – or, for an extension to the ride, turn left and see the suggestion below – then right again to return to the visitor centre. The final 2½ miles will be busier with traffic, especially in the high season.

South side of Ladybower Reservoir

There is also a 7-mile return trip possible along the south side of Ladybower Reservoir. From whichever car park you have chosen to use, follow the pavement cyclepath south along the A6013 Bamford road as far as the Ladybower Reservoir dam then turn right to cross the dam.

A. At the T-junction at the end of the dam turn right. The tarmac ends shortly and becomes a wide, stone-based track rising and falling close to the southern shores of the lake.

B. Follow this wide stone track as far as the bridge over the River Ashop. Do not be tempted to complete the circuit by using the A57 as this is a fast and busy road and no place for any but the most experienced cyclists.

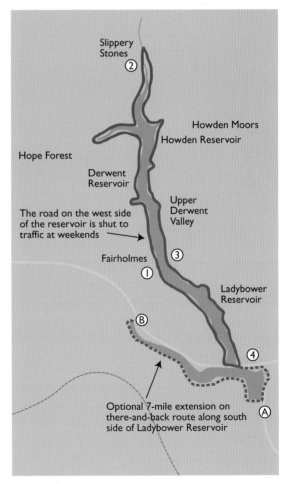

Slippery Stones
②

Howden Moors
Howden Reservoir

Hope Forest

Derwent Reservoir

Upper Derwent Valley

The road on the west side of the reservoir is shut to traffic at weekends

Fairholmes
③
①

Ladybower Reservoir

Ⓑ

④

Ⓐ

Optional 7-mile extension on there-and-back route along south side of Ladybower Reservoir

ROUTE 6
Rother Valley Country Park to Chesterfield

Distance: 3-mile circuit of the lake; a further 9 miles from the Rother Valley Visitor Centre to Tapton Lock, Chesterfield (i.e. 18 miles return).

Map/leaflet: Ordnance Survey Landranger maps 119 & 120. *The Trans Pennine Trail Map 2 (Central) – Derbyshire & Yorkshire* shows this and several other traffic-free trails in the area. See website below.

Website: www.transpenninetrail.org.uk

Hills: There are no hills.

Surface: Good quality gravel tracks.

Roads and road crossings: None.

Refreshments: Café at the Rother Valley Visitor Centre; sweets and snacks at Tapton Lock Visitor Centre.

With its craft centre, exhibitions, café, plentiful wildfowl plus a variety of rides and walks, Rother Valley Country Park is an ideal place to spend the day. A 3-mile circuit of the two lakes may be all the cycling that you want to do, but if you are interested in a longer challenge then there is a dismantled railway on the western side of the lakes that runs 6 miles south from Beighton to Staveley through a mixture of wooded cuttings and open stretches with views out into the surrounding countryside. This in turn connects to the Chesterfield Canal, taking you as far as the Tapton Lock Visitor Centre. The ride forms part of the southern link of the Trans Pennine Trail from Barnsley through Sheffield to Chesterfield and you will see a mixture of 'Route 6', 'Route 67' and 'Trans Pennine Trail' signs.

BACKGROUND AND PLACES OF INTEREST
Rother Valley Country Park

Set in 750 acres of countryside, the park offers a wide range of leisure and recreational activities on both land and water. At the centre of the park stands a historic complex of buildings based around Bedgreave Mill, now the visitor centre. Bedgreave New Mill was built near the site of earlier mills and dates from the late 1700s. The restored mill houses an exhibition which depicts the history of the area and the buildings. Next to the visitor centre is a café and craft centre.

The Chesterfield Canal

A bold and imaginative product of the early years of the Industrial Revolution, the Chesterfield Canal's prime purpose was to take Derbyshire coal to new markets. The original surveys were done by the famous canal engineer James Brindley, although he did not live to see its opening in 1777. For its time it was a magnificent piece of engineering, with the country's longest tunnel (at the time) at Norwood and one of the earliest examples of a large staircase of locks at Thorpe Salvin.

Tapton Lock

The route of the Chesterfield Canal follows the valley of the River Rother out of the town, and Tapton Lock is the first of five carrying the canal down to Staveley. The lock was constructed in 1777 and is a typical narrow lock, 72 ft long and 7 ft wide. It fell into disuse but was restored in the late 1980s. Each lock gate weighs approximately one tonne and was manufactured from solid oak at the Rochdale Canal workshops.

Starting Points & Parking:

1. **Rother Valley Country Park:** 3 miles southwest of M1, Jct 31 (Grid reference SK 453828).
2. **Chesterfield:** Tapton Lock Visitor Centre. There is car parking on the no through road (east) off the roundabout at the junction of the A61 and the A619 to the north of the Chesterfield town centre (Grid reference SK 389729).

ROUTE INSTRUCTIONS

The route is well signposted as the Trans Pennine Trail, Route 6 or Route 67.

1. Follow 'Trans Pennine Trail – Chesterfield' signs and yellow 'Doorstep Ride' signs, keeping the lake to your right. Follow the lakeside path as it swings back round to the north.

2. About 1½ miles from the start, with the water sports centre (and dinghies) opposite, you can either continue straight ahead for a circuit of the lakes or continue south to Staveley, turn left by a metal 'National Cycle Network Route 67' sign (NCN 67) and a Rother Valley Country Park information board to pass under a railway bridge, soon turning left again and following 'NCN 67' signs towards Killamarsh.

3. Follow a fine green corridor with glimpses of industrial units and factories. After almost 3 miles pass around a barrier and descend beneath power lines, then bear left uphill, signposted 'Chesterfield 7½', soon passing under a road bridge.

4. At a fork of tracks after 2 miles bear right by a low wooden post marked 'Doorstep Ride', 'Trans Pennine Trail'.

5. Join the Chesterfield Canal towpath and follow this for 4 miles to the Tapton Lock Visitor Centre. There is also the option of the 'Blue Bank Route' which runs parallel to the towpath for part of the length of the trail. Beyond the visitor centre the Trans Pennine Trail is largely on road into the centre of Chesterfield.

ROUTE 7
Clumber Park, southeast of Worksop

Distance: There are four waymarked routes of 5-10 miles (see 'Route Instructions' below).

Map/leaflet: Ordnance Survey Landranger map 120. A better option is the *Clumber Cycle Route Guide* available from the bike hire centre or from the visitor centre.

Website: www.nationaltrust.org.uk and search 'Clumber Park'.

Hills: There are several gentle hills.

Surface: A mixture of good quality gravel tracks and some rougher sections likely to be muddy in winter or after prolonged rain.

Roads and road crossings: Care should be taken crossing the estate, although none of these are very busy.

Refreshments: At the visitor centre.

Cycle Hire: At the bike hire centre (01909 476592 or 01909 484977).

Clumber Park has become one of the most popular destinations for family recreational cycling in the country, ranking alongside Rutland Water and the Peak District disused railway trails. This is due to the superb infrastructure of bike hire with all sorts of bikes and trailers available, the excellent mix of quiet estate roads, broad gravel tracks through woodlands, waymarked circuits and the beautiful setting with the lake, famous old stone bridge and chapel. There is an excellent visitor centre and café, and plenty of places to choose for a picnic or barbecue in the thousands of acres of parkland. It is also on National Cycle Network Route 6 which runs north from Derby to York; if you arrive by bike there is no entry fee to pay to get into the park.

BACKGROUND AND PLACES OF INTEREST
Clumber Park
The park is a National Trust property of some 3800 acres; Clumber House was demolished in 1938, a victim of economic decline and heavy taxation. The remains of the stable block and the Duke's Study now house the National Trust shop, restaurant and information room. Clumber Bridge was built in 1770, the lake having taken 15 years to complete. Clumber Chapel was built in 1889 for the 7th Duke of Newcastle and is a fine example of Gothic Revival architecture, described as a 'cathedral in miniature'. Limetree Avenue, the longest such avenue in Europe, was planted by the 4th Duke in 1840.

Starting Point & Parking:

Clumber Park: The car park by the bike hire centre, 4 miles southeast of Worksop (Grid reference SK 626745).

ROUTE INSTRUCTIONS

There are four suggested routes in the Clumber Cycle Route Guide and these link up with the numbered waymarks through the park:

Lakeside – 5 miles
Southern Explorer – 7 miles
Northern Fringe – 8 miles
Borders – 10 miles

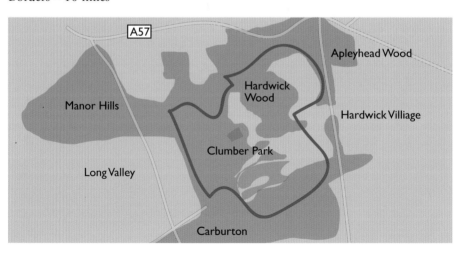

ROUTE 8
Sherwood Pines Forest, east of Mansfield

Distance: Family route (green) – 3 miles; Adventure route (blue) – 6 miles; Kitchener's Trail (red) – 8 miles (mountain bike singletrack).

Map/leaflet: Ordnance Survey Landranger map 120. More useful is the *Sherwood Pines Forest Park* cycle leaflet available from the cycle shop or the visitor centre.

Website: www.forestry.gov.uk and enter 'Sherwood Pines' in the search box.

Hills: The trails are gently undulating.

Surface: Good stone-based tracks.

Roads and road crossings: None.

Refreshments: Café at the visitor centre.

There are two well-signposted family trails through the forest and one aimed at more experienced mountain bikers. The tracks on the easier trails are wide and well maintained, so this is a good ride for cycling in a group. Sherwood Pines Forest forms part of the largest single tract of woodland in the East Midlands. Most of the forest was planted in the 1920s and 1930s in the early days of the Forestry Commission and much of the timber here has supplied local businesses, particularly as pit wood for the mining industry. In some parts of the forest the heathland vegetation, once so common in Sherwood, still exists. These areas are now being kept as heathland as part of the conservation plan. There is a Robin Hood exhibition at the visitor centre.

BACKGROUND AND PLACES OF INTEREST
Sherwood Forest

Sherwood was once a royal hunting forest, one of 90 forests or 'chases' in medieval England. At the time of William the Conqueror it covered a fifth of Nottinghamshire. The term 'forest' was a legal one, indicating an area where the Forest Laws of the medieval kings were upheld. These laws were made to protect

the valuable game and timber within the forest for the Crown. By Victorian times, the great estates of Clumber, Thoresby and Welbeck dominated north Nottinghamshire, giving the area its nickname 'The Dukeries'.

Starting Point & Parking:
Sherwood Pines car park: off the B6030, about 5 miles east of Mansfield (Grid reference SK 611638).

ROUTE INSTRUCTIONS
None are needed as the routes are very straightforward to follow.

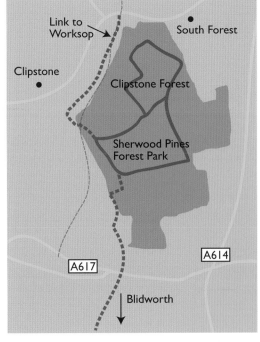

ROUTE 9
Chester to Hawarden Bridge via railway and riverside paths

Distance: (a) Railway path: 7 miles one way, 14 miles return; (b) River Dee path: 7 miles one way, 14 miles return; (c) Shropshire Union Canal: 12 miles one way, 24 miles return.

Map/leaflet: Ordnance Survey Landranger map 117. Better is the *Cycle Chester* leaflet available from www.cyclechester.com

Websites: www.cheshire.gov.uk/cycling and www.cyclechester.com

Hills: None.

Surface: Good stone-based track with the occasional short rougher section.

Roads and road crossings: Several, although none are difficult.

Refreshments: Lots of choice in Chester.

A cyclepath along the towpath of the Shropshire Union Canal links the centre of Chester to the railway path, an attractive open ride taking you from the north side of the city out into the Wirral's rich arable farmlands planted with potatoes, maize and cereal crops. The Mickle Trafford to Dee Marsh railway line once carried steel to and from the steelworks on the banks of the Dee at Hawarden Bridge. Away in the distance are the Clwydian Hills. At Hawarden Bridge you may wish to try the alternative return route to Chester by following the excellent trail alongside the River Dee (Regional Route 89) back into the centre of the city.

NB: As another option from Chester, the towpath of the Shropshire Union Canal offers a fine 12-mile ride from Waverton, southeast of Chester, through the city and north to the Waterways Museum at Ellesmere Port.

BACKGROUND AND PLACES OF INTEREST
Chester
This city of half-timbered buildings is ringed by medieval walls with fragments dating back to Saxon and even Roman times. Opposite the centre is the site of the Roman amphitheatre, and Roman archaeological finds, as well as displays on local history, can be seen at the Grosvenor Museum.

Starting Points & Parking:
1. **Chester:** Tower Gardens/the Shropshire Union Canal at the junction of South View Road and Tower Road, at the northwest corner of the city walls (Grid reference SJ 401667).
2. **Hawarden Bridge Station:** on the north side of the River Dee to the north of Connah's Quay, west of Chester (Grid reference SJ 312695).
3. For the Shropshire Union Canal you can start at the car park in **Waverton** immediately west of the canal (Grid reference SJ 454643) or at **Ellesmere Port** at the Waterways Museum (Grid reference SJ 407772).

ROUTE INSTRUCTIONS

1. From Tower Gardens in the centre of Chester at the junction of South View Road and Tower Road (at the northwest corner of the city walls) follow the towpath of the Shropshire Union Canal north towards Ellesmere Port.
2. After 1 mile, leave the canal towpath (or stay on the towpath for the ride to the Waterways Museum at Ellesmere Port) by Bridge 128B at the 'National Cycle Network Route 5' sign and turn right, up the ramp to join the railway path. Turn left for Hawarden Bridge.
3. After 7 miles you will arrive at Hawarden Bridge. Either retrace your route, or for an alternative way back to Chester follow the path on the raised embankment alongside the River Dee (Regional Route 89).
4. (River Dee option) After 7 miles, once you are back in the centre of Chester, leave the river after it makes a sharp right-hand bend, cross the A548 and join the Shropshire Union Canal towpath near Tower Road/South View Road to return to the start.

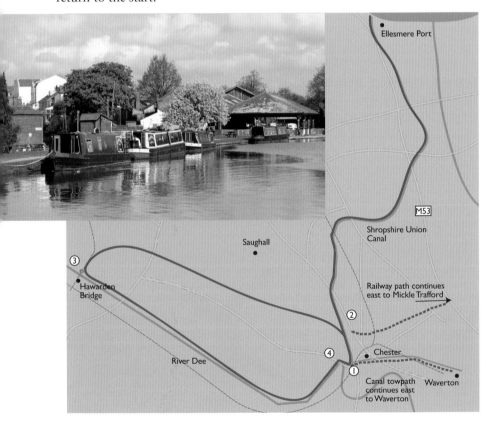

ROUTE 10
Delamere Forest, east of Chester

Distance: (a) Hunger Hill Trail, 4 miles; (b) White Moor Trail, 7 miles.
Map/leaflet: Ordnance Survey Landranger map 117.
Website: www.forestry.gov.uk/delamerehome and click on 'Cycling'.
Hills: Several gentle hills.
Surface: Good quality stone tracks.
Roads and road crossings: Care should be taken crossing the public road
that cuts through the forest. Although marked as a minor road, the traffic can
be travelling fast along it.
Refreshments: There is a café at the old station just by the main road.
Cycle Hire: At the visitor centre (01625 572681).

There are very few Forestry Commission holdings of any size in the area covered by this book – you would need to go to Wales or Yorkshire for that – but whilst Delamere Forest Park is not particularly large, it does have two waymarked cycle routes which are ideal for family cycling: broad gravel tracks with a few gentle hills but nothing really to worry about. Starting from the visitor centre, the ride crosses and recrosses the railway line, passing through mixed broadleaf and conifer woodland, with a fine display of wildflowers in the spring and early summer. You twice have to cross a road running east-west through the forest and although it is marked as a minor road on the map, the traffic can be travelling fast so take great care on both crossings.

BACKGROUND AND PLACES OF INTEREST
Delamere Forest
The woodlands were once the royal hunting preserve of the Earls of Chester – the visitor centre has displays of Delamere's history. The forest is noted for kestrels, sparrowhawks, foxes and badgers.

Starting Point & Parking:
Delamere Forest Visitor Centre car park: situated just off the B5152, close to Delamere railway station, 7 miles south of Runcorn and 9 miles east of Chester (Grid reference SJ 548704).

ROUTE INSTRUCTIONS
The two routes are well signposted.

1. From the car park by the Delamere Forest Visitor Centre return towards the public road and take the first left over a bridge with a 'No entry' (for cars) sign.

You will come to an obvious crossroads of tracks where you have a choice:

(a) The Hunger Hill Trail, 4 miles, blue arrows, to the right;

(b) The White Moor Trail, 7 miles, white arrows, to the left.

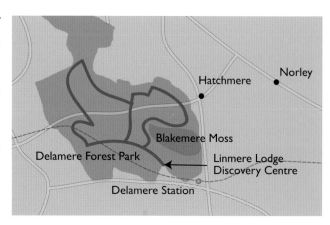

ROUTE 11
Canals through Stoke

Distance: (a) Trent & Mersey Canal – Harecastle Tunnel to Barlaston: 10 miles one way, 20 miles return; (b) Caldon Canal – Etruria Museum to Stockton Brook: 7 miles one way, 14 miles return.

Map/leaflet: Ordnance Survey Landranger maps 118 and& 127. Much more useful for Stoke is the *Stoke-on-Trent Cycling Map & Guide*. See website below.

Website: www.stoke.gov.uk/cycling

Hills: None.

Surface: Good stone-based track with the occasional short rougher section.

Roads and road crossings: None.

Refreshments:

1. Trent & Mersey Canal: Café at Etruria Industrial Museum; Plume of Feathers pub, Barlaston; lots of choice just off the route.
2. Caldon Canal: Foxley Hotel and Millrace pub, Milton.

BACKGROUND AND PLACES OF INTEREST

The Trent & Mersey Canal can be followed on a good quality towpath from the southern portal of Harecastle Tunnel (on the northern edge of Stoke) all the way through the centre of the city and south to the Plume of Feathers pub at Barlaston. The Caldon Canal, linking to the Trent & Mersey at the Etruria Museum, offers the option of a further 7-mile ride heading northeast from the centre of Stoke to the A53 at Stockton Brook. Signs of Stoke's industrial past are ever present, but this ride also offers the real sense of a green corridor through the city.

NB: With a Stoke cycling map (see below) it is possible to work out a link from the Caldon Canal near Milton to the southern end of the Biddulph Valley Trail (Ride 14).

Starting Points & Parking:

1. **Bathpool Park:** close to the southern end of the Harecastle Tunnel on Lowlands Road, a minor road linking the A34 to the A527 to the south of Kidsgrove (Grid reference SJ 841520).
2. **Westport Lake:** just east of the A500 to the northwest of Stoke city centre (Grid reference SJ 858498).
3. **Etruria Industrial Museum:** Lower Bedford Street, west of the city centre, at the junction of the two canals (Grid reference SJ 873468).
4. **Barlaston:** Plume of Feathers pub, on the Trent & Mersey Canal between Stoke and Stone, east of the A34 (Grid Reference SJ 887384).

ROUTE INSTRUCTIONS

1. From the Bathpool Park car park (at the south end of the park), exit onto the minor road (Lowlands Road), turn left and use the pavement cyclepath as far as the mini-roundabout. Turn right, then right again onto a track leading down to the canal towpath at the southern end of Harecastle Tunnel.

2. Follow the canal south past Westport Lake, then after a further 3 miles you come to the junction of the Trent & Mersey Canal and the Caldon Canal at the Etruria Industrial Museum. At this point you can either continue south on the Trent & Mersey or divert east on the Caldon Canal for 7 miles to Bridge 25 at Stockton Brook (the towpath starts near an arched metal footbridge).

3. (South on the Trent & Mersey Canal). Follow the towpath past Stoke railway station and south for a further 5 miles to the Plume of Feathers pub at Barlaston. Shortly beyond this point the quality of the towpath deteriorates.

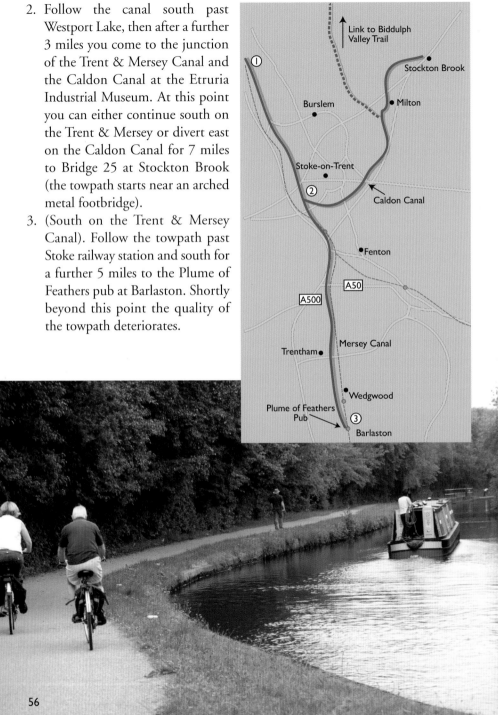

Distance: Up to 18 miles each way. The flattest section runs for 12 miles between Middleton Top, Parsley Hay and Sparklow.

Map/leaflet: Ordnance Survey Landranger map 119. A leaflet is available from the Peak District National Park Office (01629 816200).

Website: www.peakdistrict.gov.uk/cycle

Hills: The whole trail is a climb from High Peak Junction (near Matlock) northwest to Sparklow. The section from Matlock up to Middleton Top is exceedingly steep and not recommended for any but the fittest of cyclists. From Middleton Top on to Sparklow there is a 165ft/50m climb.

Surface: Good stone-based track with the occasional short rougher section.

Roads and road crossings: Several. Care should be taken at the crossing of the A5012 east of Friden.

Refreshments: Soft drinks and sweets at the cycle hire/visitor centres; Royal Oak pub at Sparklow (northwest of Parsley Hay); Rising Sun pub is just off the route in Middleton.

This is one of the best known and most popular routes in the country, offering a superb challenge in the heart of the Peak District from High Peak Junction (south of Matlock) via Middleton Top and Parsley Hay to Sparklow. The trail runs through the limestone scenery of the White Peak and links with the Tissington Trail in the north at Parsley Hay, 10 miles southeast of Buxton. If you start at the western end of the trail, remember it is all downhill on the outward leg.

NB: Unless you are experienced and fit, it is suggested you go no further east than the Middleton Top Visitor Centre (i.e. do not go down to High Peak Junction in the valley) as there are two very steep sections needing very good brakes on the way down and very strong legs on the way back up.

BACKGROUND AND PLACES OF INTEREST
The old railway
The 33-mile Cromford & High Peak Railway was one of the earliest railways in the country, built between 1825 and 1830. In the early days, horses were used to haul waggons along the rails.

Starting Points & Parking:
1. **Parsley Hay:** there is a large pay & display car park and cycle hire centre here, just off the A515 about 10 miles southeast of Buxton (Grid reference SK 147637).
2. **Friden:** near the junction of the A515 and A5012 (Grid reference SK 172607).
3. **Middleton Top Visitor Centre:** southwest of Matlock on the B5035 towards Ashbourne (Grid reference SK 276552).
4. **High Peak Junction:** on the A6 south of Matlock (Grid reference SK 315561). This last option is not recommended unless you are super-fit.

ROUTE INSTRUCTIONS
None are needed as the route is linear and impossible to miss. If you wish to link to the Tissington Trail this can be done at Parsley Hay, at the northwest end of the High Peak Trail.

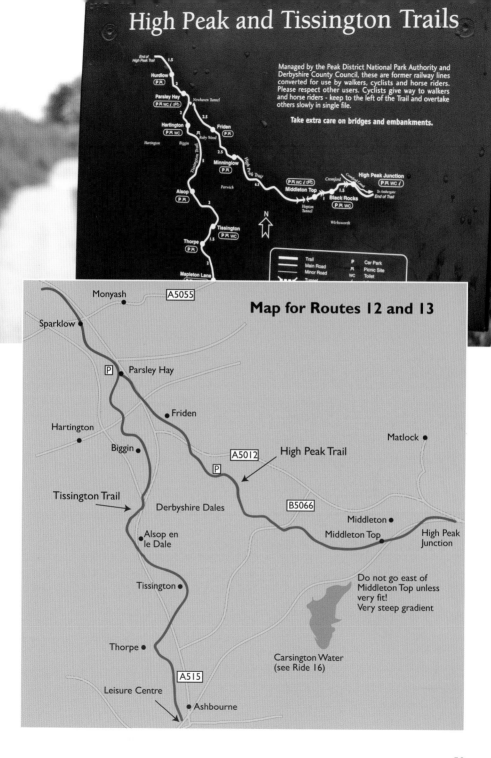

High Peak and Tissington Trails

End of
High Peak Trail 1.5

Hurdlow
P ☐ 2

Parsley Hay
P ☐ WC / 🚲 Newhaven Tunnel

2.5

Hartington   Friden
P ☐ WC   P ☐

Hartington   Biggin   Ruby Wood

2.5

Minninglow
P ☐

Tissington Trail   High Peak Trail   Parwich

Alsop   4.5
P ☐

3   Cromford   Cromford Canal   High Peak Junction
        P ☐ WC / 🚲   P ☐ WC / 🚲
Middleton Top   1.5   To Ambergate
Tissington   Black Rocks   End of Trail
P ☐ WC   P ☐ WC

Thorpe   Hopton   Wirksworth
P ☐   Tunnel

Mapleton Lane

Managed by the Peak District National Park Authority and
Derbyshire County Council, these are former railway lines
converted for use by walkers, cyclists and horse riders.
Please respect other users. Cyclists give way to walkers
and horse riders - keep to the left of the Trail and overtake
others slowly in single file.

Take extra care on bridges and embankments.

N

	Trail		P	Car Park
	Main Road	☐	Picnic Site
	Minor Road	WC	Toilet
	Tunnel		

Map for Routes 12 and 13

Monyash   A5055

Sparklow

P   Parsley Hay

Friden

Hartington   Matlock

Biggin   A5012   High Peak Trail

Tissington Trail   P

Derbyshire Dales   B5066

Middleton
Alsop en   Middleton Top   High Peak
le Dale   Junction

Tissington   Do not go east of
Middleton Top unless
very fit!
Very steep gradient

Thorpe

Carsington Water
(see Ride 16)

Leisure Centre   A515

Ashbourne

ROUTE 13
Tissington Trail, north of Ashbourne

Distance: 13 miles one way, 26 miles return.

Map/leaflet: Ordnance Survey Landranger map 119. A leaflet is available from the Peak District National Park Office (01629 816200).

Website: www.peakdistrict.gov.uk/cycle

Hills: There is a steady drop of almost 700ft (215m) from Parsley Hay to Ashbourne. For this reason it is worth starting at Ashbourne when you are fresh, riding uphill towards Parsley Hay, leaving you with a downhill on the way back.

Surface: Good stone-based track with the occasional short rougher section.

Roads and road crossings: None.

Refreshments: Plenty of choice in Ashbourne; soft drinks and sweets at the cycle hire/visitor centres; Dog & Partridge pub in Thorpe and the Waterloo Inn in Biggin are just off the route; coffees and teas at Bassett Wood Farm, Tissington.

Together with the High Peak Trail, this is one of the most famous railway paths in the Peak District, if not the whole country. Passing through neat pastures bounded by drystone walls and the dramatic limestone scenery of the Derbyshire Dales, including several rock cuttings, it climbs gently up from Ashbourne to Parsley Hay, setting you up for a fantastic descent. If you ever need to persuade a non-cyclist of the joys of cycling, drop them at the top and pick them up at the bottom! If you are at the other end of the spectrum in terms of fitness and experience, there are now waymarked routes along lanes through the villages of Tissington, Bradbourne and Hopton linking the Tissington Trail, Carsington Water and the High Peak Trail and offering a tough, full day challenge.

Starting Points & Parking:

1. **Ashbourne:** the trail starts from the far end of the leisure centre car park on the west side of town (off the A515 Lichfield road) near the Station Hotel/Beresford Arms Hotel on Station Road (Grid reference SK 177465).

2. **Ashbourne:** bike hire centre at Mapleton Lane (Grid reference SK 177469).

3. On the minor road east of **Thorpe** (Grid reference SK 166503).

4. On the A515 near **Alsop en le Dale** (Grid reference SK 157549).

5. Car parks on the B5054 east of **Hartington** (Grid reference SK 151611).

6. **Parsley Hay:** there is a large pay & display car park at the cycle hire centre (Grid reference SK 147637).

ROUTE INSTRUCTIONS

None are needed as the route is very straightforward to follow. See map on page 59.

ROUTE 14
Biddulph Valley Trail, north of Stoke

Distance: 10 miles one way, 20 miles return.

Map/leaflet: Ordnance Survey Landranger map 118. Much more useful for Stoke is the *Stoke-on-Trent Cycling Map & Guide*. See website below.

Website: www.stoke.gov.uk/cycling

Hills: The route climbs north from Stoke to Biddulph, then drops gently to Congleton.

Surface: Tarmac or good stone-based track.

Roads and road crossings: Toucan crossing of the B5051 Ford Green Road on the northern edge of Stoke. Several more minor roads to cross.

Refreshments: Lots of choice just off the route in Biddulph and Congleton.

Starting from Holden Lane Pools on the northeast outskirts of Stoke, the raised trackbed of the old Biddulph Valley Line provides fine views towards the Peak District. The ride climbs past an old colliery and from a highpoint near Biddulph drops down through woodland to pass beneath a magnificent viaduct close to Congleton. NB: With the aid of a Stoke cycling map (see below) it is very easy to link the southern end of this ride to the Caldon Canal (Ride 11).

BACKGROUND AND PLACES OF INTEREST
The old railway
The Biddulph Valley Line was opened in 1859 and as Congleton's main arterial link with the Potteries it provided the town's economic lifeblood with the movement of freight of every description from straw to war weapons. It lasted 109 years, the final train running in 1968. In 1980 Congleton Borough Council bought the line from British Rail and it was put into service once again to provide recreation for local people and a refuge for wildlife.

Starting Points & Parking:
1. **Stoke:** the trail starts from the Holden Lane Pools car park on the south side of the A53 Leek road, about 3 miles northeast of the city centre (Grid reference SJ 893501).
2. **Biddulph:** leave the A527 Congleton to Stoke road at the traffic lights at the southern end of Biddulph, turning on to Newpool Road, signposted 'Mow Cop/Brown Lees'. The trail starts beneath the railway bridge after 200 yards (Grid reference SJ 878568).

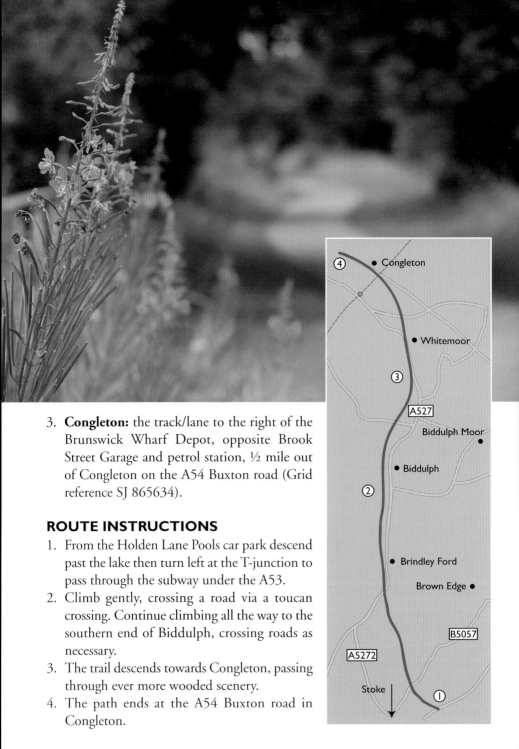

3. **Congleton:** the track/lane to the right of the Brunswick Wharf Depot, opposite Brook Street Garage and petrol station, ½ mile out of Congleton on the A54 Buxton road (Grid reference SJ 865634).

ROUTE INSTRUCTIONS

1. From the Holden Lane Pools car park descend past the lake then turn left at the T-junction to pass through the subway under the A53.
2. Climb gently, crossing a road via a toucan crossing. Continue climbing all the way to the southern end of Biddulph, crossing roads as necessary.
3. The trail descends towards Congleton, passing through ever more wooded scenery.
4. The path ends at the A54 Buxton road in Congleton.

64

Distance: 8 miles one way, 16 miles return.

Map/leaflet: Ordnance Survey Landranger map 119. A leaflet is available from the Peak District National Park Office (01629 816200).

Website: www.peakdistrict.gov.uk/cycle

Hills: Gentle climb north and south of the lowest point of the trail at the confluence of the rivers Hamps and Manifold at Weags Bridge.

Surface: Tarmac or good stone-based track.

Roads and road crossings: There is one busy road (the A523) to cross at Waterhouses. The trail uses a short section of quiet lane for about 1½ miles.

Refreshments: The Manifold Inn at Hulme End; various tea shops and refreshment vans along the way; Ye Olde Crown Hotel at Waterhouses.

The Manifold Trail is one of the most popular in the Peak District. The scenic railway path follows the course of two rivers – the Manifold and the Hamps – from Waterhouses (west of Ashbourne) via Wettonmill to Hulme End. The Manifold appears and disappears: during the drier months it takes an underground course, leaving just the dry, stony river bed and tree-lined banks. High above the wooded hillsides are accessible caves. The Manifold Trail dips in the middle, at the junction of the rivers Hamps and Manifold, so there is a gentle climb from this point (Weags Bridge) north to Hulme End or south to Waterhouses.

BACKGROUND AND PLACES OF INTEREST
The old railway
The Leek & Manifold Valley Light Railway was opened in 1904, closed in 1934 and converted to recreational use in 1937. It was a narrow-gauge railway designed by E. R. Calthrop, who had tested and proved his ideas on the Barsi Light Railway in India.

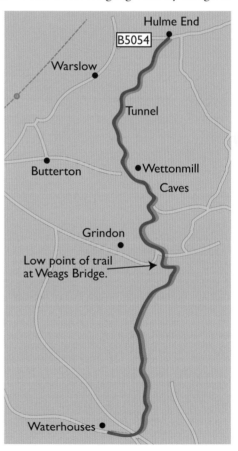

Starting Points & Parking:
1. **Hulme End:** 12 miles southwest of Bakewell. Turn off the B5054 just to the west of the Manifold Inn (Grid reference SK 103594).
2. **Waterhouses:** 9 miles northwest of Ashbourne. Turn off the A523 Ashbourne to Leek road at Ye Olde Crown Hotel in Waterhouses, signposted 'Cauldon Lowe, Manifold Track'. Go under the bridge and immediately left into the car park (Grid reference SK 085501). To get to the start of the trail go to the far end of the car park and follow the waymarks.

ROUTE INSTRUCTIONS
None are needed as the route is very straightforward to follow.

ROUTE 16
Carsington Water, northeast of Ashbourne

Distance: 8-mile circuit.

Map/leaflet: Ordnance Survey Landranger map 119. A better option is the free map available from the visitor centre (01629 540696).

Website: www.carsingtonwater.com

Hills: There are several short, steep hills on the far side of the lake from the visitor centre.

Surface: Good quality gravel tracks.

Roads and road crossings: Care should be taken on the two crossings of the B5035. There is a 1-mile section on minor lanes through Hopton.

Refreshments: Café at the visitor centre; Miners Arms pub between Hopton and Carsington on the far side of the lake.

Cycle Hire: At the visitor centre (01629 540478).

One of the country's most recently built reservoirs, Carsington Water has quickly established itself as a major focus for recreational cycling, offering a circuit around the lake which is demanding enough to give young children a real sense of achievement when they complete the ride. There are two crossings of the B5035 and about one mile is spent on a minor road, but as the latter runs parallel with the main road, very few vehicles have any reason to use it. This lane detour to the lovely stone-built village of Hopton enables you to enjoy a stopping point at the pub about three-quarters of the way around the circuit.

BACKGROUND AND PLACES OF INTEREST
Carsington Water

Although planning for the reservoir started in the 1960s, the final go-ahead was not given until 1979. Work was at an advanced stage when part of the original dam collapsed in 1984. The dam was then levelled to its foundations and work on a new design was started in February 1989. Construction was finished in 1991 and the reservoir and visitor centre were opened by the Queen in 1992. Most of the water in the reservoir is pumped from the River Derwent when the river level is high. The reservoir is the ninth largest in England – when at its highest level it can hold 7,800 million gallons.

Starting Point & Parking:

Carsington Water Visitor Centre: pay & display car park, just off the B5035 about 5 miles to the northwest of Ashbourne (Grid reference SK 242517).

ROUTE INSTRUCTIONS

1. With your back to the visitor centre entrance, turn left then at the corner of the building and continue straight ahead on the broad gravel track.

2. Follow this obvious track with the water to your left, crossing the dam wall, following the frequent signposts.

3. The route becomes hillier! At the main road (B5035) TAKE CARE crossing onto the minor lane opposite. Follow the waymarks through the village of Hopton, past the Miners Arms pub.

4. At the second crossing of the B5035 TAKE CARE as you go straight ahead towards the car park, then bear right at the fork and follow this track for 2 miles back to the start.

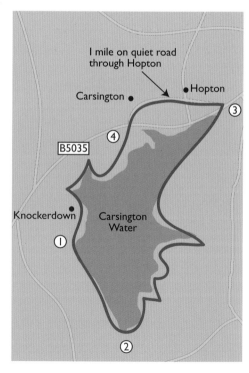

Distance: (a) Pleasley Trails: 5-mile circuit; (b) Silverhill Trail: 4 miles one way, 8 miles return; (c) Five Pits Trail: 6 miles one way, 12 miles return (i.e. up to 25 miles in total if you do all three rides).

Map/leaflet: Ordnance Survey Landranger map 120. The *Five Pits Trail* map is available from the website below

Website: www.derbyshire.gov.uk and search for 'Five Pits Trail'.

Hills: Several climbs, especially on the Five Pits Trail.

Surface: Good stone-based track with the occasional short rougher section.

Roads and road crossings: Several, although none are difficult.

Refreshments: Carnarvon Arms pub, Fackley, just off the route, near Teversal; teas at the Teversal Visitor Centre; Wheatsheaf pub in Tibshelf.

There is an ever growing network of trails on the old mineral railways on the Nottinghamshire/Derbyshire border, offering a chance to see the transformation and greening over of these old mining areas. The Pleasley Trails are three separate railway paths lying between Pleasley, Skegby and Teversal, linked together to form a circular route.

Deep cuttings show the exposed limestone rock of the area. The Five Pits Trail follows the course of the railway that used to serve the collieries between Grassmoor and Tibshelf Ponds, passing through rolling countryside with fine views. There are several hills, which may come as a surprise to anyone expecting railway paths to be flat! One is near the start and another near to Tibshelf. The Silverhill Trail links these two trails. You may also wish to explore the spur that leads to Brierley Forest Park, lying just to the south of the trail, or other shorter trails coming off the main routes, namely the Rowthorne and Stockley Trails to the west and northwest of Pleasley or the Meden Trail to the east.

BACKGROUND AND PLACES OF INTEREST
The old railway lines
The railways used in this ride were opened in 1892 to serve the expanding coalfield and were operated initially by the Midland Railway Company's mineral line and later by the Great Central Railway Company. The railway served the five pits of Tibshelf, Pilsley, Holmewood, Williamthorpe and Grassmoor. By 1971, the collieries it served had closed, causing the closure of the railway. Pilsley coal received royal patronage when Queen Mary (consort of George V) chose to burn nothing but 'Pilsley Brights' on her drawing room fire at Buckingham Palace.

Starting Points & Parking:

1. **Pleasley Pit Country Park:** Pit Lane, Pleasley, just off the A617/B6417/B6407 roundabout about 3 miles northwest of Mansfield (Grid reference SK 502645).

2. **Skegby:** the Teversal Trail car park, on Buttery Lane, just off the B6014 Mansfield to Tibshelf road, signposted 'Manor Estate' (Grid reference SK 495614).

3. **Teversal Visitor Centre:** just off the B6014 between Sutton and Tibshelf, west of Mansfield (Grid reference SK 479614).

4. **Grassmoor Country Park:** car park between Temple Normanton and Grassmoor, southeast of Chesterfield. Take the A617 Mansfield road out of Chesterfield for 4 miles. Turn off south onto the B6245, then take the B6039, following signs for 'Temple Normanton' and 'Holmewood'. Turn second right. The car park is ¾ mile along this road on your right (Grid reference SK 413673).

ROUTE INSTRUCTIONS
Pleasley and the Teversal Trail Circuit

1. Leave the Pleasley Pit Country Park car park heading back towards the main road, then turn right opposite the start of the low wall on the left and a red-brick house with white columns (number 4) through a wooden barrier onto the railway path. The path turns right, parallel with the road.

2. Pass through several rock cuttings. There is one steep descent with loose gravel where you should take care. About 2½ miles after leaving Pleasley you will arrive at the car park at Skegby. Retrace your steps for 300yds, then at the fork of tracks bear left, signposted 'Silverhill Trail'.

3. After 1 mile, you will arrive at a track junction close to the Teversal Visitor Centre (well worth a visit).

4. There are several junctions and signs near here (see Silverhill Trail below for a longer ride). For a short ride, follow 'Teversal Track' signs back towards Pleasley. After almost 1½ miles, at the junction with a lane, turn right, then left to drop back down onto the railway path.

5. After about ½ mile, at a T-junction of tracks just after an information board and the junction with the Rowsley Trail, turn right to return to the Pleasley Pit Country Park car park.

Silverhill Trail

A. From the Teversal Visitor Centre head past the old mining artefacts to the barrier. Turn left, then shortly left again following 'Silverhill Trail' and 'Tibshelf' signs.

B. The ride passes beneath the M1, then under a high red-brick bridge and descends to finish at the bridleway that connects Blackwell to Stonebroom. Retrace your route back towards Teversal Visitor Centre/Pleasley, or, for a longer ride, about 1.3 miles from the turnaround point turn left onto...

Five Pits Trail

C. Go past the Tibshelf Ponds. Keep bearing right. After ¾ mile cross the road via the toucan crossing in Tibshelf near the church and the Wheatsheaf pub.

D. Drop down into, then climb up out of, the valley formed by Westwood Brook. Follow signs for Five Pits Trail, Pilsley and Grassmoor, dropping steeply down to the woodland of Locko Plantation.

E. Keep bearing left, crossing roads as necessary (and passing under two sets of power lines) to descend to Grassmoor Country Park car park, located to the northeast of the village of Grassmoor. Retrace your route.

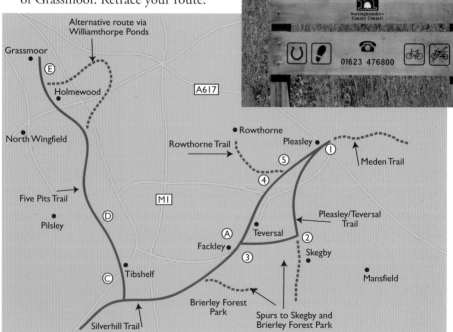

ROUTE 18

Cloud Trail from Derby south to Worthington

Distance: 13 miles one way, 26 miles return.

Map/leaflet: Ordnance Survey Landranger maps 128 & 129. An excellent map called *Cycle Derby* shows this and several other trails in the area. For the latest information about cycling in Derby and cycle leaflets covering the city call the Cycle Derby Team (01332 715054).

Website: www.cyclederby.co.uk

Hills: There are no hills.

Surface: Good quality gravel tracks.

Roads and road crossings: Two busy roads in Derby are crossed safely via toucan crossings. There is a short road section if you wish to go for refreshments in Worthington.

Refreshments: Lots of choice in Derby; also in Melbourne (1 mile off the route); Bull's Head pub, Wilson; Malt Shovel pub, Worthington (¾ mile on quiet roads beyond the end of the trail).

Starting from the very heart of Derby, the trail follows an attractive riverside path, canal towpath and a disused railway on its way from the urban centre into the heart of the countryside. As the route becomes more rural in nature you will come across some beautifully painted Millennium Mileposts and some very fine stone sculptures. The ride ends at Worthington, which has a curious red-brick octagonal lock-up and a pub at the far end of the village. There is the option of visiting the vast quarry that lies just to the northeast of Worthington.

NB: There is also an option of staying close to the River Derwent and following this traffic-free path east to Elvaston Country Park where there are several trails around the parkland.

BACKGROUND AND PLACES OF INTEREST

Swarkestone
The village lies half a mile from the Trent & Mersey Canal, beside the River Trent. Its bridge and causeway date back to the 13th century and are reputed to be the southernmost point Bonnie Prince Charlie reached on his march to London.

Breedon on the Hill
On a limestone bluff above the village stands the Norman church of St Mary and St Hardulph with its magnificent 8th-century Saxon frieze, Iron Age hillfort and views of the Trent valley.

Starting Points & Parking:
1. **Derby:** Riverside Gardens in the centre of town (near the bus station and the Eagle Centre Market).
2. **Worthington:** from the crossroads in the village by St Matthew's Church follow Breedon Lane downhill, signposted 'Cloud Trail', then shortly turn first right and follow this to the car park (Grid reference SK 406210).

ROUTE INSTRUCTIONS
1. The ride starts in the Riverside Gardens in the centre of Derby (near the bus station and the Council House). Follow signs for the Riverside Path and stay close to the river for 2 miles. (An alternative option at the start is to follow National Cycle Network Route 6 on the north side of the river; shortly after passing the Derby Telegraph buildings, cross to the south side of the river via a footbridge with white railings).

2. Go past Pride Park, the stadium of Derby County Football Club, pass beneath a low black bridge (with attached pipe!) then take the second of two closely spaced paths to the right by a brightly painted cast-iron Millennium signpost. Turn right onto National Cycle Network Route 6.

3. Keep following signs for Swarkestone, Melbourne and National Cycle Network Route 6, crossing several roads.

4. Pass beneath the A50, cross a bridge over the Trent & Mersey Canal, then turn left onto the towpath, signposted 'Melbourne'.

5. After 1½ miles, just before the large metal bridge over the canal, bear right and join the railway path, soon crossing the River Trent.

6. After 4 miles the path veers right and runs parallel with the A42. Cross the bridge over the dual carriageway, then bear left to rejoin the railway path.

7. After 1½ miles, shortly after a stone 'egg' sculpture, the trail forks: go left to see the vast quarry or right/straight on to visit Worthington. For the village, go through the car park, turn left onto the minor lane, then at the crossroads at the end of Breedon Lane turn left onto Church Street, signposted 'Griffydam, Osgathorpe'. Follow this road through the village for ¾ mile past the octagonal red-brick lock-up to the Malt Shovel pub.

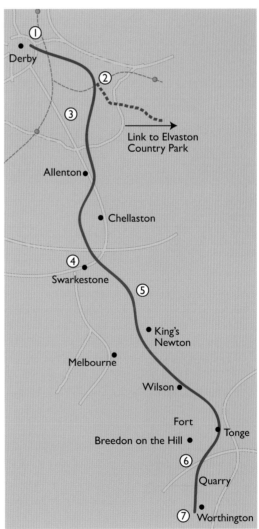

ROUTE 19
River Trent through Nottingham

Distance: 12 miles one way, 24 miles return.

Map/leaflet: Ordnance Survey Landranger map 129. There are also two good cycling maps (north and south) produced by Nottingham City Council covering the city. See website below for details.

Websites: www.nottinghamcity.gov.uk and www.nottinghamshire.gov.uk

Hills: None.

Surface: Good stone-based or tarmac track.

Roads and road crossings: No difficult road crossings – Trent Bridge is crossed on the pavement, having passed underneath it.

Refreshments: Tea room and Steamboat Inn, Trent Lock; café just off the route at Attenborough Nature Reserve; Boathouse Café at Beeston Marina; café at National Watersports Centre.

The River Trent can be followed for 12 miles almost entirely traffic-free, passing close to the centre of Nottingham on a journey northeast from Trent Lock (south of Long Eaton) to the National Watersports Centre at Holme Pierrepont. The first few miles are predominantly rural, passing alongside a series of lakes in the Attenborough Nature Reserve. From Clifton Bridge through to the Nottingham Forest Football Club the route has a much more urban feel. Beyond the football club and rowing clubs the trail opens up again on its way towards the National Watersports Centre, where you may well see kayakers battling with water rushing over weirs, or rowers out practising on the rowing lake.

BACKGROUND AND PLACES OF INTEREST
The Big Track
A 10-mile circular route following the River Trent and the Nottingham Canal through the centre of the city. This is described in a small booklet called *The Big Track*. Details of the route are available from **www.thebigwheel.org.uk**.

Starting Points & Parking:
1. **Trent Lock:** southwest of Nottingham (Grid reference SK 489313).
2. **Central Nottingham:** Trent Bridge (Grid reference SK 581383).
3. **National Watersports Centre** (Grid reference SK 681389).

ROUTE INSTRUCTIONS
South to north, from Trent Lock to the National Watersports Centre:

1. From the free car park at Trent Lock make your way towards the River Trent past the 'Steamboat Inn' signpost. Cross the footbridge over the Erewash Canal towards the Lock House tea room and turn right alongside the River Trent (with the water to your right).
2. Follow the wide gravel path past Nottingham Yacht Club, then past a series of lakes on your left. At a junction of tracks shortly after a wooden swing gate turn right following signs for 'Riverside Path, Beeston Marina, Nottingham'. (Remember this point for the return trip.)

3. Go past the Beeston Marina Boathouse Café, then immediately after Beeston Locks cross the canal via a wooden bridge (No 20) and continue straight ahead to rejoin the River Trent path (i.e. do not turn left along the Beeston Canal).

4. Go past Grove Farm sports ground onto a quiet road, then on a left-hand bend just before a large road bridge turn right off tarmac, following signs for 'Trent Valley Way'.

5. After ½ mile the path bears left away from the river to join a shared-use pavement alongside the busy Queens Drive. (Take good note of this junction for your return trip as it is easy to miss.) Rejoin the riverside path beyond the ornate red-brick bridge.

6. Go past parkland and the war cemetery on your left. Shortly after passing under an ornate blue metal bridge (Trent Bridge) turn sharp left back on yourself to cross the bridge via the pavement and join the riverside path on the south side of the river, running past Nottingham Forest Football Club and a series of rowing clubs.

7. Continue for a further 2 miles until you arrive at the National Watersports Centre. It is suggested you turn around at this point, following 'Trent Valley Way' and 'Riverside Path to Beeston Marina/Trent Lock' signs back to the start.

ROUTE 20
Nutbrook Trail from Shipley Country Park to Long Eaton, west of Nottingham

Distance: 10 miles one way, 20 miles return.
Map/leaflet: Ordnance Survey Landranger map 129.
Websites: www.derbyshire-peakdistrict.co.uk/shipleypark.htm or www.derbyshire.gov.uk and search 'Country Parks'.
Hills: There is one hill, near the country park.
Surface: Good quality gravel tracks.
Roads and road crossings: Only if you go into Long Eaton.
Refreshments: At Shipley Country Park; lots of choice in Long Eaton.
Cycle Hire: At Shipley Country Park (01773 719961).

Shipley Country Park has many fine tracks within its landscaped parkland. Should you not feel up to a 20-mile there-and-back ride to Long Eaton there are plenty of shorter options within the park itself. Once you have negotiated your way up and down the hill at the start you find yourself on a railway path that runs along the course of the old Stanton Branch Line for five miles down to the Erewash Canal, linking Eastwood with the River Trent at Trent Lock, south of Long Eaton. You pass many fine red-brick buildings along the banks of the canal before the trail drops you in the middle of Long Eaton.

BACKGROUND AND PLACES OF INTEREST
Shipley Country Park
Located on the edge of Heanor and Ilkeston, less than 10 miles from Derby, Shipley Country Park offers 600 acres of attractive, varied landscape and 1,000 years of history. Shipley was developed in the 18th century as a country estate and coal mining area by the influential Miller-Mundy family. Following the demise of the old coal mines and opencast quarries, former railways have been transformed into leafy pathways, old reservoirs are now tranquil lakes teeming with wildlife, and reclaimed spoil heaps are now large woodlands, rolling hills and wildflower meadows. The park was opened in 1976.

Starting Points & Parking:
1. **Shipley Country Park:** off the A608/A6007 to the west of Nottingham (Grid reference SK 431452).
2. **Long Eaton (southwest of Nottingham):** by Asda and the Council Offices. Turn off the roundabout on the A6005 in the centre of Long Eaton onto Midland Street, signposted 'Superstore, Town Hall, Sandiacre Cycle Route' (Grid reference SK 491339).

ROUTE INSTRUCTIONS

From Shipley Country Park you are following signs for 'Nutbrook Trail', 'Sandiacre', 'Long Eaton' and 'National Cycle Network Route 67'.

1. From the information board in the car park at Shipley Country Park take the gravel track signposted 'Public bridleway, Osborne Pond'. At a crossroads of tracks go straight ahead into woodland, soon bearing right to join the railway path. There is a pond to your right.

2. The track surface becomes tarmac. At the junction of roads immediately after the Lakeside Business Centre (on your right), turn right downhill. Continue in the same direction, staying on the tarmac path, at one point jinking left then right. Climb, then descend.

3. Go past a lake. At the T-junction turn right, then shortly take the first tarmac track to the left opposite a red-brick house.

4. After 2 miles follow the tarmac path as it turns sharp right, then sharp left, soon passing under two railway bridges.

5. After almost 3 miles, at the canal turn right (remember this point for the return route).

6. Easy to miss! After 3 miles, by Dockholme Lock and a hump-back red-brick bridge, turn left by a Nutbrook Trail signpost onto a path running parallel with the towpath.

7. Follow the trail as it swings left past a tall red-brick chimney, passing through a barrier then turning right onto a tarmac path. The trail ends near Asda and the Town Hall in the centre of Long Eaton.

Heanor
Shipley Park
67 🚲

Sandiacre
Long Eaton
67 🚲

Heanor ①
●
Shipley ②
Country Park ●
③
Ilkeston ●
④
Kirk Hallam ●
⑤
Sandiacre ●
⑥
Long Eaton ⑦
●

ROUTE 21
Silkin Way, south of Telford

Distance: 5 miles one way, 10 miles return. The ride can be extended at its southern end by following the River Severn west to Ironbridge (2 miles) or south to Bridgnorth (8 miles).

Map/leaflet: Ordnance Survey Landranger map 127. *The Walking & Cycling Map of Telford & Wrekin* is available from the website below.

Website: www.telford.gov.uk (search 'Cycling').

Hills: Several gentle climbs.

Surface: Tarmac or good quality gravel tracks.

Roads and road crossings: Several crossings of minor roads.

Refreshments: Lots of choice in Telford; Hot Metal Café near entrance to Blists Hill; café at China Museum, Coalport; Brewery Inn, Woodbridge Inn at Coalport.

This ride runs through the heart of the area where the Industrial Revolution started. The iron bridge over the River Severn at (unsurprisingly!) the village of Ironbridge was a major step on the route which saw Great Britain rise to industrial pre-eminence throughout the world in the late 18th century and 19th century. The iron wheel used as the motif for the Silkin Way is an indication of the area's industrial past. The route starts in the heart of the New Town of Telford and follows a dismantled railway for much of its course, passing through deep rock cuttings and thickly wooded stretches. The River Severn is reached at Coalport, where there is a pub on the other side of the lovely bridge over the river. From here you can head west parallel with the river towards Ironbridge or south towards Bridgnorth.

BACKGROUND AND PLACES OF INTEREST
The Birthplace of the Industrial Revolution
At Coalbrookdale in 1709, Abraham Darby started to experiment with methods of smelting iron ore using coke instead of charcoal. From his modest beginnings as a maker of iron-bellied pots and household pans, Darby's clever innovations were later used to create monsters! Two of these iron monsters, David and

Sampson, now feature in the Open Air Museum at Blists Hill. They are two mighty furnace engines that together gave sterling service for just over a century, pumping air into the Prioslee furnace, like a giant pair of bellows.

Starting Points & Parking:
1. **Telford Town Park:** (follow brown tourist signs) in the centre of town, which lies about 1 mile southeast of the M54, Jct 5 (Grid reference SJ 700082).
2. **Coalport:** the China Museum, on the road alongside the River Severn, parallel with the A442 to the south of Telford, south of the M54, Jct 4 (Grid reference SJ 698024). The Silkin Way is accessed opposite the Brewery Inn.

ROUTE INSTRUCTIONS

The route is signposted with an iron wheel logo.

1. From the Town Park car park in the centre of Telford go into the park through the green metal gates and continue straight ahead along a road with humps and a white painted cycle lane (pass to the left of the Wonderland theme park).

2. Leave the park, ignoring the car parks to the left, and take the next left downhill by a black metal barrier and a wooden 'Silkin Way' signpost, then shortly right. Soon after, at a fork of tracks, bear right downhill to join the railway path. Take good care to remember this point for the return trip.

3. Pass beneath several bridges, following signs for 'National Cycle Network Route 55, The Gorge and Blists Hill'.

4. About 3 miles after leaving Town Park, the course of Silkin Way runs on the pavement alongside the main road, crossing the approach road to Blists Hill Victorian Town (there is a good café here, just before the entrance). Continue past Blists Hill and follow the pavement as it bears left away from the road.

5. Follow the trail past the Brewery Inn and onto a continuation of the path, then bear right to arrive at the end of the path at Coalport Bridge and the Woodbridge Inn.

6. If you wish to visit Ironbridge, cross the bridge over the River Severn and turn sharp right, signposted 'Severn Valley Way', following this for 2 miles. For Bridgnorth cross the bridge and turn left after the Woodbridge Inn.

Return

Follow signs for 'National Cycle Network Route 55' and 'Telford Town Centre' back along the outward route. Towards the end of the return trip, at the green metal gates at the entrance to Town Park, by a Withy Pool information board, continue straight ahead back to the start, ignoring the left turn on National Cycle Network Route 55.

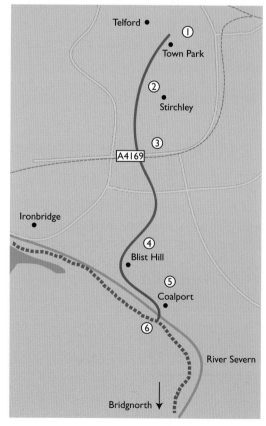

ROUTE 22
Cannock Chase, southeast of Stafford

Distance: The Sherbrook Valley Route is 12 miles long. There are several shorter options.

Map/leaflet: Ordnance Survey Landranger maps 127 & 128. *The Cannock Chase Cycling Map* can be purchased from the visitor centre.

Websites: www.forestry.gov.uk and search 'Cannock Chase'; www.chasetrails.co.uk and www.cannockchaseaonb.org.uk

Hills: There are several hills. The ride is mainly downhill in the first half and uphill in the second half.

Surface: A mixture of good quality gravel tracks with some rougher sections.

Roads and road crossings: Care should be taken crossing the two roads on the circuit. There is a short section on a minor road.

Refreshments: Good café at the visitor centre. There is a pub in Little Haywood, just to the north of the lowest point of the ride (at the bottom of Sherbrook Valley, near Instruction 3).

Together with the woodland around Sherwood Forest, Cannock Chase is the largest Forestry Commission holding in the area covered by this book. In character it is far from the dense blocks of conifers that cloak hillsides in Wales and Scotland – there are many open, sandy spaces, a pleasant mixture of broadleaf and coniferous trees and, more important from the cyclist's point of view, a large network of bridleways, many of which are well-drained broad, stone-based tracks where it is possible to cycle all year round. The ride described is a waymarked route through the forest. Waymarkings are always a blessing because it is notoriously difficult to give adequate route directions to guide people through a forest where the only noticeable features are trees, tracks and hills! The ride is largely a descent in the first half down the course of Sherbrook Valley and largely a climb in the second half up Abraham's Valley.

NB: It is essential to buy the cycling map for Cannock Chase as it shows all the cycling trails and enables you to work out where you are. Without this you are likely to get lost. Mountain bikes are recommended.

BACKGROUND AND PLACES OF INTEREST
Cannock Chase
The chase is a remnant of a vast royal hunting forest. At 17,000 acres it is the smallest mainland Area of Outstanding Natural Beauty in Britain. Much of Cannock Chase is recognised by English Nature as a Site of Special Scientific Interest.

Starting Point & Parking:
Birches Valley Visitor Centre: 2 miles southwest of Rugeley (Grid reference SK 018171).

ROUTE INSTRUCTIONS

1. The trail starts between Swinnerton Cycle and Go Ape. Follow the green arrows past Fairoaks Pools.

2. Cross Birches Valley Road and Penkridge Back Road, heading northwest to join the top of the Sherbrook Valley.

3. Keep following the waymarked trail down the valley then across Stepping Stones towards the car park on the A51.

4. The trail heads back south and climbs steadily for over 2 miles, recrossing the two roads and rejoining the outward route past Fairoaks Pools back to the start.

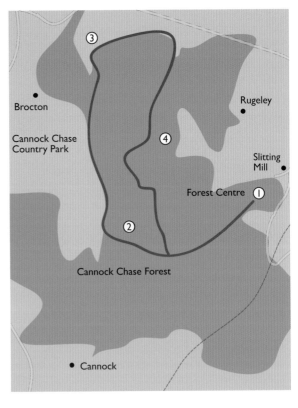

Distance: 3½ miles one way, 7 miles return.

There are also rides in the newly created Donisthorpe Woodland Park:

Green route – Woodland Park Circular – 1.5 miles

Purple route – Hill Street Circular – 1.1 miles

Orange route – Moira Road Circular – 1 mile.

Map/leaflet: Ordnance Survey Landranger map 128.

Website: www.leics.gov.uk/ashby_cycle_info.pdf

Hills: There are no hills.

Surface: Good quality gravel tracks.

Roads and road crossings: There is one road to cross.

Refreshments: Lots of choice in Measham; Furnace Tearooms at Moira Furnace; cafés at the two Conkers Visitor Centres; Navigation Inn on the B5004 to the northeast of Overseal, at the end of the trail.

The signboards along this short railway path ride to the northeast of Measham offer a clear explanation not only of the area's industrial history but also of the huge efforts needed to restore nature's balance after more than 150 years of dumping mining and industrial waste without considering the long-term environmental consequences. As a result of these huge efforts, lakes, grassland and woodland have been created where before there were stagnant, hazardous pools and a moonscape of spoils. Within a generation the area will be covered by mature trees and a visitor would never know what was previously there. In addition to the 7-mile there-and-back ride along the railway path there are three different circuits of between 1 and 2 miles in what is now called Donisthorpe Woodland. The ride also includes a visit to Moira Furnace and the Conkers Centre, set in the heart of the new National Forest.

BACKGROUND AND PLACES OF INTEREST
Ashby & Nuneaton Joint Railway
Opened in 1873, the railway was built to transport coal from the local pits to London and the South East. The line closed to regular passenger traffic in 1931, and the last goods train ran in 1981.

Bath Pit
This pit was sunk in 1806 and closed in 1854. Whilst sinking the shaft the miners hit a saline spring at a depth of 600ft. This became the source of Moira Spa. However, many people were put off by the proximity to the colliery, so a new bath house was built at Ashby-de-la-Zouch. It was completed in 1826 and thrived for many years using Moira water.

Moira Furnace
The furnace opened in 1806 to extract iron ore from the coal deposits already being mined in the Ashby Woulds area. However, it remained operational for only 11 months due to the variability in quantity and quality of the product.

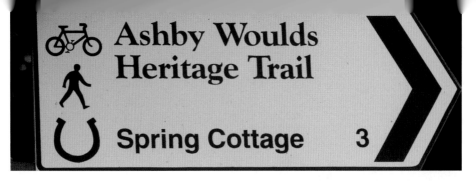

Ashby Woulds Heritage Trail

Spring Cottage   3

Measham

The town developed around mining interests in the 19th and 20th centuries and became one of the principal centres of the Industrial Revolution, mainly as a result of the efforts of Joseph Wilkes, who bought the manor in 1777. He was a banker, a coal mine owner, a brick producer and mill owner. He introduced the first steam engine in the area for his mill.

Starting Point & Parking:

Measham: the library car park in the centre of town just off the M42/A42 to the northeast of Jct 11, about 9 miles southeast of Burton upon Trent (Grid reference SK 332119).

ROUTE INSTRUCTIONS

1. From the car park by the library in the centre of Measham follow the 'Ashby Woulds Heritage Trail' signposts.
2. After ¾ mile turn left to join the pavement alongside the road that passes beneath the A42, then shortly, at the next Heritage Trail signpost, turn right to rejoin the railway path.
3. Follow the trail into Donisthorpe Woodland. After about 300yds of gentle descent, turn right off the railway path by a 'National Cycle Network Route 63' signpost onto a similar wide gravel path, following signs for 'Spring Cottage via Moira'. At the T-junction with the canal turn left.
4. Go past Moira Furnace, then cross the road onto a continuation of the canal towpath.

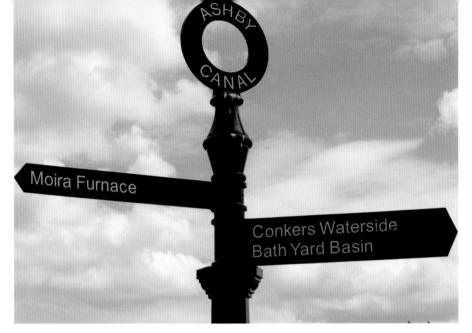

5. Go through the Conkers Waterside car park and bear left* onto a gravel path, then turn left to cross the railway line.

   *or to visit the main Conkers Visitor Centre continue straight ahead through the tunnel – the visitor centre is a few hundred yards along this trail.)

6. At the junction with the railway path, turn left to return to Measham (or right to visit the Navigation Inn on the B5004).

7. Rejoin the outward route and follow it back to the start.

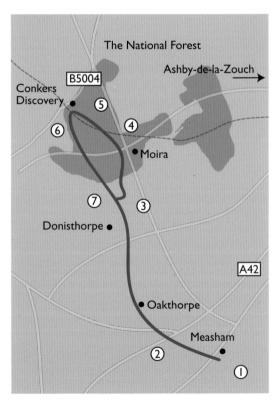

The National Forest

Ashby-de-la-Zouch →

B5004

Conkers Discovery

⑤

⑥

④

● Moira

⑦

③

Donisthorpe ●

A42

● Oakthorpe

Measham
●

②

①

ROUTE 24
River Soar north from Leicester

Distance: Central Leicester to Watermead Country Park – 4 miles one way, 8 miles return. There are several circuits possible within Watermead Country Park itself.

Map/leaflet: Ordnance Survey Landranger map 140.

Websites: www.leics.gov.uk/country_parks_watermead or www.leicester.gov.uk and follow links through 'Transport & Streets' to 'Cycling'.

Hills: None.

Surface: Tarmac or good stone-based track, occasionally narrow alongside the river.

Roads and road crossings: There are two road crossings, the busier one (Abbey Park Road) via a toucan crossing.

Refreshments: Gazebo Café in the abbey grounds; café at the National Space Centre; White Horse pub, Birstall.

The valley of the River Soar through Leicester offers a largely traffic-free corridor from Watermead Country Park in the north through to Abbey Park in the centre of the city then south to Blaby, either via the Great Central Way (a railway path) or via the Grand Union Canal. This ride focuses on the northern section, from the landscaped gardens of Abbey Park past the Space Centre (there is a rocket inside!) and alongside the river into Watermead Country Park, where there is a chance of exploring a whole network of trails around the watercourses and lakes, including a climb up a hill to see a sculpture of a mammoth.

BACKGROUND AND PLACES OF INTEREST
National Space Centre
Take a journey through the six hands-on galleries, stopping at over 150 interactive experiences, then travel in the glass lifts through three floors in the 42m high Rocket Tower. Sit back in the UK's largest planetarium, the Space Theatre, as you go on a voyage of discovery in the 360° fulldome experience.

Watermead Country Park

A 140-hectare haven for wildlife, the park is developing one of the largest reedbed areas in the Midlands and five bird hides, including a two-storey hide, provide great viewing spots for visitors. It is a wetland area with over 12 lakes and smaller ponds. Running through the park are the River Soar and Grand Union Canal, which provide an essential corridor for wildlife.

Starting Points & Parking:

1. **Central Leicester:** St Margaret's Pasture car park near the sports centre, just off St Margaret's Way, near Abbey Park (Grid reference SK 584054).
2. **Watermead Park:** north of Leicester, near the junction of the A46 and A607 (Grid reference SK 608114).

ROUTE INSTRUCTIONS

1. From the car park by the sports centre in Abbey Park follow the tarmac path around the perimeter of the five-a-side football pitch to cross the concrete bridge over the River Soar, then turn right (north), soon arriving at the large ornate building housing the tea rooms.

2. Follow signs for Watermead Park and Riverside Way, with the river to your right. Cross Abbey Park Road via a toucan crossing. Go past the National Space Centre. At the next road (Thurcaston Road) turn right to cross the bridge, then turn left to rejoin the riverside path, with the river now to your left.

3. Continue alongside the river/canal and into Watermead Country Park. There are many trails around the lakes, which may seem confusing, but the area is bounded on three sides by housing or dual carriageways so you can't get too lost! There is a sculpture of a mammoth at the top of a small hill which is worth climbing up to see.

A46
③ Watermead Country Park

There are many miles of gravel tracks in Watermead Country Park, suitable for cycling

Birstall

A563

National Science Centre

Abbey remains

Abbey Park

②

①

Leicester

Distance: 17 miles for the circuit, plus 7 miles for the Hambleton peninsula.
Map/leaflet: Ordnance Survey Landranger map 141. The cycle hire outlets also have maps.
Website: www.anglianwater.co.uk/leisure/what-to-do/cycling
Hills: There are several short climbs.
Surface: Tarmac or good stone-based track.
Roads and road crossings: There are several short road sections on quiet lanes. The longest is to the east of Manton where you should take extra care if you are with children.
Refreshments: Cafés at the visitor centres; Horse & Jockey pub in Manton at the southwest corner of the lake.

Britain's favourite reservoir cycle route offers a superb day out around the largest man-made lake in Western Europe, covering an area of 3,100 acres. The ride uses a good all-year-round track with some tarmac sections and links Egleton (near Oakham), Manton, Edith Weston, Whitwell and Upper Hambleton. The visitor centres all have something of interest: tropical butterflies, exotic insects and fish at the Empingham Leisure Centre, the Normanton church and Water Museum at Normanton Leisure Centre, and the Drought Garden at Barnsdale. There are three short sections on public roads: the section along the lane which leads from the A606 near Oakham to the Hambleton peninsula is fairly quiet, likewise the lane to Egleton. There is a busier 1-mile section east of Manton, but much of this is either on a parallel cyclepath or on a designated cycle lane.

NB: For people looking for a shorter ride, the best bit of the circuit runs from Whitwell Centre on the north shore via the dam at the east end of the lake to the Normanton Centre at the southeast corner of the lake (or vice versa).

BACKGROUND AND PLACES OF INTEREST
Rutland Water Nature Reserve

This is one of the most important wildfowl sites in the country, at times holding in excess of 20,000 waterfowl. The reserve occupies a narrow strip of land running for nine miles around the western end of the reservoir. It is also home to the successful Osprey Project: the first osprey chick to fledge in central England in 150 years was hatched here in 2001. Ospreys are regularly seen fishing over the reservoir from April to September.

Starting Points & Parking:

The car parks are all located along the eastern half of the lake: clockwise from the north, there are pay & display car parks at Barnsdale, Whitwell, Empingham and Normanton visitor centres. Rutland Water lies between Oakham (A606/A6003) and Stamford (A1).

ROUTE INSTRUCTIONS

The route is best ridden anti-clockwise to minimise right turns. It is just after turning off the cyclepath alongside the A606 (east of Oakham) that you have the choice of adding another 7 miles to your trip by completing a circuit of the Hambleton peninsula.

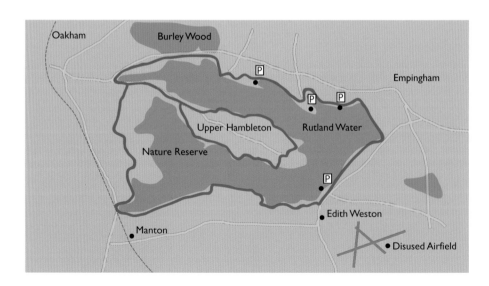

ROUTE 26
Kingswinford Railway Walk, west of Birmingham

Distance: 8 miles one way, 16 miles return.
Map/leaflet: Ordnance Survey Landranger map 139.
Website: http://wmcycling.webs.com/southstaffsrailwaytrail.htm
Hills: There are no hills.
Surface: Good stone-based track with the occasional short rougher section.
Roads and road crossings: None.
Refreshments: Tea shop at Wombourne station; pubs just off the route.

Despite its proximity to the conurbation of Wolverhampton, this ride along the disused railway of the Kingswinford Line has a very fine wooded, countryside feel to it. The trail is in reasonable condition between Aldersley Stadium and Wombourne. Along its whole length the trail runs parallel with the Staffordshire & Worcestershire Canal. Indeed you have the option of extending your ride northwards by following the canal towpath for a few miles before it becomes rougher and narrower. Although the old railway line continues south of Wombourne, it soon becomes very muddy and/or rough.

BACKGROUND AND PLACES OF INTEREST
The old railway line
The railway was built by the Great Western Railway Company as the Kingswinford Branch Railway (a branch off the Worcester to Wolverhampton Main Line). The line opened in 1925, but was not very successful and had only a relatively short working life.

Staffordshire & Worcestershire Canal
The canal runs for 46 miles from Great Haywood near Stafford to Stourport on the River Severn. One of the original Brindley canals, it opened in 1772 and was one of the main routes to the north from Birmingham before the Shropshire Union Canal was built.

Starting Points & Parking:
1. **Wombourne:** turn off the A449 Wolverhampton to Kidderminster road at the roundabout near Wombourne (at the junction with the A463) signposted 'Kingswinford Railway Walk'. Follow signs for Trysull onto Billy Buns Lane, then just before a brown and cream coloured railway bridge turn right onto a track signposted 'Kingswinford Railway Walk' (Grid reference SJ 870940).
2. **Aldersley Stadium:** 2 miles northwest of Wolverhampton city centre between the A41 and the A449 (Grid reference SJ 897007).

ROUTE INSTRUCTIONS
North from Wombourne
1. From the car park turn right onto the railway path. Continue for 3 miles to Castlecroft and a further 3 miles to Aldersley Stadium.
2. At Aldersley Leisure Village (Hugh Porter Way) you can either retrace your steps or link to the Staffordshire & Worcestershire Canal towpath. To get to the canal, turn right downhill towards the car parking area, then opposite the visitor centre turn left on a wide tarmac path by a yellow metal barrier signposted 'National Cycle Network Route 81'.
3. Follow the perimeter of the five-a-side football pitch (on your right) to join the canal. Here you can:

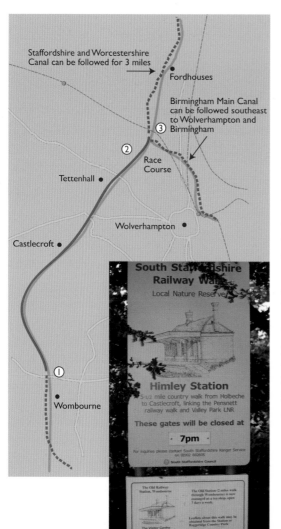

(a) turn left to follow the Staffordshire & Worcestershire Canal for 3 miles as far as the A449 at Coven Heath;

(b) turn right to follow the Staffordshire & Worcestershire Canal as an alternative return route back to Wombourne;

(c) cross the bridge over the canal onto the towpath of the Birmingham Main Line Canal alongside Wolverhampton Locks to go into the centre of Wolverhampton (and on towards Birmingham).

South from Wombourne
The railway path soon deteriorates and is only fit for mountain bikes and mud lovers! It can be followed south then east for 3½ miles towards Pensnett as far as a set of wooden steps by a car crusher's yard.

ROUTE 27
Canals of Birmingham

Distance: (a) Birmingham to Wolverhampton – 14 miles one way, 28 miles return; (b) Birmingham to King's Norton Tunnel – 6 miles one way, 12 miles return.
Map/leaflet: Ordnance Survey Landranger map 139. *The Birmingham Cycling & Walking Map* is available from the website below. Also useful is the Wolverhampton Bike Map (www.wolverhampton.gov.uk/cycling)
Website: www.birmingham.gov.uk/transportation
Hills: None.
Surface: The Worcester & Birmingham Canal towpath is a good quality gravel track. The first section of the Birmingham to Wolverhampton Canal towpath is very good, but there are also some rough sections.
Roads and road crossings: None.
Refreshments: Cafés and pubs in the centre of Birmingham and Wolverhampton.

The canals were the first transport system especially designed to carry goods around the country. Birmingham was and still is at the heart of the national network, and the hub of the canal network in the city lies around Digbeth Basin and Gas Street Basin. To the northwest the ride along the canal towpath from Birmingham to Wolverhampton, known simply as the Birmingham Canal or the Main Line, is a trip past the sinews of a muscular, industrial city with metal foundries and hot metal smells. The route to the south ends at King's Norton Tunnel, one of the longest in the country. On its way south it passes the tall, ornate, red-brick clocktower of Birmingham University and Cadbury World at Bournville.

NB: You will need to walk your bike through the Edgbaston Tunnel and be aware of any other users as the towpath is narrow between the railings and the tunnel wall. It is best to take lights for the Coseley Tunnel on the route to Wolverhampton.

BACKGROUND AND PLACES OF INTEREST
The Main Line Canal from Birmingham to Wolverhampton

By 1769, the engineer James Brindley had completed the first of Birmingham's canals from Wednesbury to Newhall, then to a wharf, beyond Gas Street Basin, where the Holiday Inn now stands. By 1772, the Old Main Line extended to Wolverhampton. The canal created rapid growth in industry – coal and building supplies were brought in and manufactured goods carried out. In the next half century the canal system spread rapidly and expanding trade brought great congestion. In the 1820s Thomas Telford constructed a straight canal, the New Main Line, running parallel at a lower level to the Old Main Line. Despite advances in canal planning, the Galton Valley cutting was still dug out by men using picks, shovels and wheelbarrows.

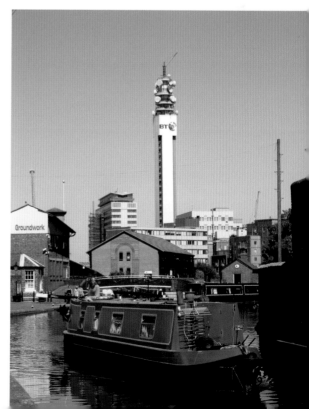

Starting Points & Parking:

Birmingham: Gas Street Basin in the centre of the city. The towpath to the south ends at King's Norton Tunnel (also known as Wast Hill Tunnel) which is located near the junction of Shannon Road and Primrose Hill in the Hawkesley/Walker's Heath area (Grid reference SP 048780).

Wolverhampton: the railway station on the east side of the ring road.

ROUTE INSTRUCTIONS

(a) From the centre of Birmingham to Wolverhampton. With your back to the National Indoor Arena turn right, with the water to your left. There are occasionally paths on both sides of the canal. Keep an eye out for the signs indicating where you change sides. The path can be followed for up to 14 miles to Wolverhampton, including the long and dark Coseley Tunnel.

(b) From the centre of Birmingham along the Worcester & Birmingham Canal to King's Norton Tunnel. Start from the Gas Street Basin in the centre of Birmingham. Follow signs for the Worcester & Birmingham Canal for 6 miles as far as King's Norton Tunnel.

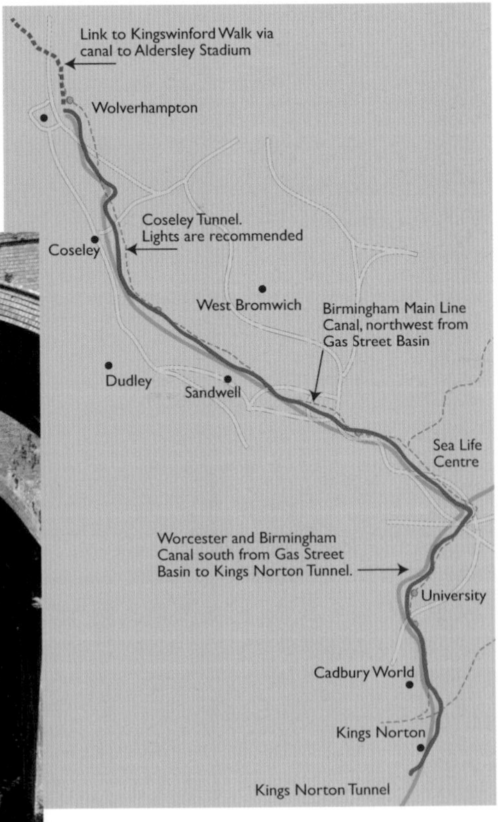

Link to Kingswinford Walk via canal to Aldersley Stadium

Wolverhampton

Coseley Tunnel. Lights are recommended

Coseley

West Bromwich

Birmingham Main Line Canal, northwest from Gas Street Basin

Dudley

Sandwell

Sea Life Centre

Worcester and Birmingham Canal south from Gas Street Basin to Kings Norton Tunnel.

University

Cadbury World

Kings Norton

Kings Norton Tunnel

ROUTE 28

Brampton Valley Way, south of Market Harborough

Distance: 14 miles one way, 28 miles return.
Map/leaflet: Ordnance Survey Landranger maps 141 & 152.
Website: www.northamptonshire.gov.uk or www.leics.gov.uk and search 'Brampton Valley Way'.
Hills: None.
Surface: Good stone-based track.
Roads and road crossings: Several, although none are difficult.
Refreshments: Lots of choice in Market Harborough; Waterloo Farm tea room about 2 miles south of Market Harborough; Windhover pub at the southern end of the route on the A5199 to the south of Chapel Brampton.

The Brampton Valley Way is the longest dismantled railway path in the region, connecting Market Harborough with the outskirts of Northampton and forming part of National Cycle Network Route 6, which runs all the way from London to Keswick in the Lake District. It is a wide, well-maintained trail with few barriers, making it a perfect 'conversational' ride: a chance to catch up with friends while getting some exercise. The trail includes two tunnels where you will need lights. There are some fascinating old steam locomotives and rolling stock at Chapel Brampton.

NB: As a suggestion for another ride in the area, the towpath of the Market Harborough Arm of the Grand Union Canal can be followed for 6 miles northwest from Market Harborough to Foxton Locks.

BACKGROUND AND PLACES OF INTEREST

The old railway line

The railway line was closed in 1981 and was purchased by Northamptonshire County Council in 1987. It opened for recreational use as the Brampton Valley Way in 1993. It is named after the tributary of the River Nene – the Brampton Arm – the valley which it follows for much of its length.

Starting Points & Parking:

1. **Market Harborough:** from the traffic lights in the centre of town follow the A508 Northampton road for ½ mile. The Bell Inn is on your left. The cyclepath starts at the back of the pub (Grid reference SP 737867).

2. **Northampton:** from the centre of town follow the A508/A5199 north towards Leicester for 4 miles. Shortly after the end of the built-up area and the start of the countryside, turn right on Brampton Lane, signposted 'Boughton', then right again into the car park (Grid reference SP 737653).

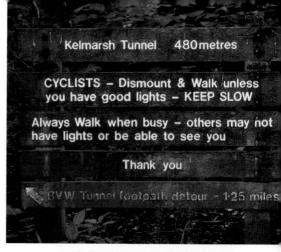

ROUTE INSTRUCTIONS

1. (Starting from the Bell Inn, Market Harborough) It is not hard to follow the course of the railway line south towards Northampton as it is almost all intact. There are several road crossings.

2. It is suggested you go only as far as the Windhover pub on the A5199, just beyond the old Pitsford & Brampton railway station. Beyond here the trail soon becomes much rougher.

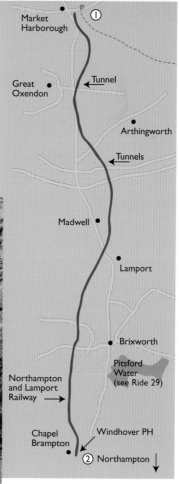

ROUTE 29
Pitsford Water, Brixworth Country Park, north of Northampton

Distance: 7-mile circuit of the lake.
Map/leaflet: Ordnance Survey Landranger maps 141 & 152. Much more useful is the map you can get from Pitsford Water Cycle Hire (01604 881777) near the visitor centre.
Website: www.anglianwater.co.uk/leisure/what-to-see/water-parks/pitsford
Hills: There are no hills.
Surface: Good quality gravel tracks.
Roads and road crossings: The pavement is used on the road across the causeway.
Refreshments: Café at the visitor centre.
Cycle Hire: Pitsford Water Cycle Hire (01604 881777).

This trail around Pitsford Water is a model of its kind, keeping you close to the water for the whole circuit on well-maintained paths, avoiding time spent on roads, which is so often the failing of circuits around reservoirs. The lake is popular with swans, anglers and windsurfers; if the wind is blowing strongly you may well witness some pretty amazing acrobatics by top class windsurfers whizzing over the surface of the lake and turning on a sixpence! Nearby is the Brampton Valley Way, a 14-mile railway path between Northampton and Market Harborough, so if you are left with a taste for more cycling after completing the circuit of the lake, why not try the railway path as well?

BACKGROUND AND PLACES OF INTEREST
Pitsford Water
Pitsford Water was built in 1956 to supply Northampton and is now managed by Anglian Water. Brixworth Country Park has been developed to include special gardens and ponds, tracks suitable for disabled access and a link to the Brampton Valley Way.

Starting Point & Parking:
Pitsford Water Visitor Centre: Brixworth Country Park, off the A508, about 6 miles north of Northampton (Grid reference SP 753695).

ROUTE INSTRUCTIONS
From the visitor centre, head downhill towards the masts of the dinghies. At the main track around the reservoir you can turn right or left as the circuit is signposted in both directions and there is no obvious advantage one way or the other. The dam is at the western end of the circuit, close to the visitor centre; at the eastern end, the cycle trail uses the causeway across the water.

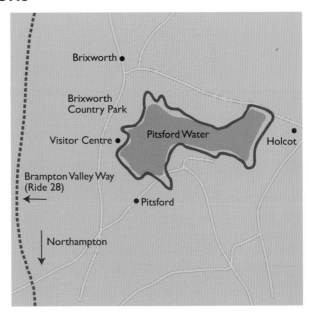

ROUTE 30
Stratford Greenway, southwest of Stratford-upon-Avon

Distance: 5 miles one way, 10 miles return.
Map/leaflet: Ordnance Survey Landranger map 151.
Website: www.warwickshire.gov.uk and put 'Stratford Greenway' into the search box.
Hills: None.
Surface: Good stone-based track
Roads and road crossings: One by the Milcote car park
Refreshments: Lots of choice in Stratford; café in railway carriage near the start and in railway carriage about halfway along (just after road crossing and second car park); Mason's Arms pub and post office/shop, Long Marston.

This popular ride is flat and wide, offering a good opportunity to have a chat with friends and family whilst taking a bit of exercise. It is difficult to give exact instructions to get to the car park at the start, so if you are arriving at the trail for the first time ensure you have a good map and be patient! The trail soon runs past the race course and a bike hire centre, operating out of an old railway carriage. Stannals Bridge over the River Avon looks like it was made from a Meccano set! The ride continues southwest through a rich agricultural landscape with clumps of broadleaf woodland dotted amongst the fields. Long Marston offers the opportunity of a pub as a turnaround point before heading north back to the cultural delights of Stratford.

BACKGROUND AND PLACES OF INTEREST
The old railway
Built in 1859 by the Oxford, Worcester & Wolverhampton Railway and later absorbed by the Great Western Railway, the line linked Stratford and the Midlands to Cheltenham and the South West. Finally, as part of British Rail, it carried the 'Cornishman' to and from the West Country until the line was closed in 1976.

Stratford-upon-Avon
Renowned as the birthplace of Shakespeare, this well-preserved market town is a showcase of Tudor architecture, its broad streets lined with half-timbered houses.

Starting Points & Parking:
1. **Stratford-upon-Avon:** the car park on the southern edge of town at the start of the trail. Follow signs for A4390 and Shipston on Stour to get to the roundabout where the trail starts (Grid reference SP 196540).
2. **If coming from** outside Stratford it may be better to start from the Milcote car park about halfway along the trail on the minor road between Welford-on-Avon and Clifford Chambers (Grid reference SP 171515).

ROUTE INSTRUCTIONS

1. Finding the start of the railway path will be far more difficult than following it as the trail is linear with no deviations as far as Long Marston.

2. If you wish to visit the Mason's Arms pub in Long Marston you will need to follow signs for the 'Village shop and post office' near the end of the trail (4½ miles from the start) which will bring you out on Wyre Lane, almost opposite the pub.

3. If you go right to the end of the trail you will arrive at Station Road, which is busier and further from the pub. If you wish to visit Long Marston it is best to retrace your steps on the railway path for ½ mile back towards Stratford, then turn left.

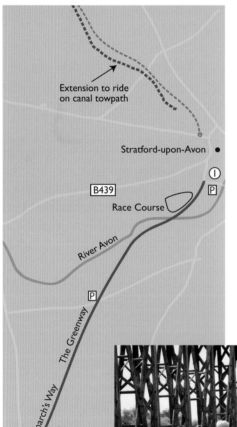